Reiki Reflections

Reiki Reflections

Sharing the Light, Changing Hearts!

Rev. Cheryl-Ann M. Case

To order additional copies of this book, contact:
Xlibris
1-888-795-4274
www.Xlibris.com
Orders@Xlibris.com
747478

I dedicate this book to Dr. Mikao Usui and Mrs. Hawayo Takata. They have guided, protected and assisted me in every way possible. I only wish I could have met you in person!

Disclaimer

Reiki Reflections: Sharing the Light, Changing Hearts may contain information that opposes traditional beliefs and is considered controversial. This is not meant to offend anyone. These diary entries are from the author's personal experiences and spiritual perspective. If you think you recognize yourself in these entries, the similarities are strictly coincidental unless I have received your specific written permission to use your name in the story. The author is not a medical Practitioner and in no way is providing medical advice or diagnosis, and therefore, strongly encourages anyone with symptoms of depression or medical conditions to seek professional help. Reiki in combination with your doctor's advice and follow up is highly recommended for optimal healing. The information provided is strictly for informational purposes and the author is not responsible for any actions taken by the reader.

Foreword

One of my first memories of money happened at the age of eleven. I remember being in Woolworths with Mom and wanted to buy a diary. She told me I couldn't have one as she had no extra money to spend on it. I was so mad that I couldn't get it that day! Instead, I got it as a Christmas present. I was so happy to see this small red book with gold edged pages with a lock! Looking back, I can say Mom probably knew that diaries started on January 1 back then and figured it could wait. I started my first diary on January 1, 1975 and have kept diaries since then! I was so disappointed that I didn't get one right away as I must have intuitively known how important they would be one day.

When I first started giving Reiki to people, I never dreamed this could be the passion of my life! It started with just me, then just my family and friends. Before you know it, I was giving Reiki to anyone who wanted it! I started using "sharing the light" as a sign off on emails, and felt it was really a part of who I want to be, a light worker. Sharing the light, everywhere I can! It wasn't until becoming a Reiki Master did I understand that I was also changing hearts. Those who hesitated at first had a change of heart, and suddenly realized MAYBE there IS something to healing naturally! I LOVE the AH-HA moments! That in itself is the reason I continue to give Reiki. It is more fulfilling to my soul than any amount of money in the world!

I apologize to those who I may offend with my stories, as that is not my intention. Reiki is love, and my main goal is to encourage more people to use Reiki on a daily basis for personal transformation! This book is my journey of awakening with Usui Reiki. Although I believed in God before Reiki, I did not feel him in my heart or understand how to get him there mentally. (I prefer to refer to God as him in this book.) I never had the proper education on divine knowing through my limited Catholic upbringing. I was only at the level of praying to them, not working with them. This was something I wanted to have, and finally with Reiki, I went from a skeptic to true believer! Reiki brought me everything I needed, including my direct connection to God, Jesus, Archangels and guides. This connection did not happen quickly, as it is not necessary to connect with anything nor believe in any religion in order to give Reiki. Universal Life Force Energy will do the work alone. For years, I gave Reiki after calling on my guides to help. And then in 2015, I found additional information that propelled me into deeper healing sessions with the help of Jesus. Although I refer to Jesus, please change it to who brings love to your heart, and the process described may accomplish the same goal for you.

I want you to know that I have respect for your beliefs and hope that you will respect mine. I try to find God everywhere and in everything and keep him in the forefront of my thoughts. I am very spiritual and give thanks and worship wherever I am. Plants and trees in nature, walking on a treadmill or the sea shore, looking at my husband and children or my Reiki clients all bring me a sense of love for life and oneness with God! Many of my friends are from different religious faiths and all found their true purpose in healing with Reiki. Reiki works with all religious beliefs, bringing you to a higher level of devotion.

Reiki and hindsight are 20/20. You may not understand the importance of each small lesson along the way; then, if you have been keeping journals or diaries, you can reflect and see the big picture! I would have said, "No, I am not doing that," and simply shut it down had I known all the experiences I had to go through to be the Reiki Master I am now. Of course, when I am looking back, it all makes sense. This is my journey, the ups and downs of it. There are plenty of books on how to do Reiki; this is not that type of book. This was written for all Reiki Practitioners and masters. I wish I had something like this when I first started learning Reiki in the late 1990's. There were times I thought I was imagining things and yelled out for help. There were other times I knew things from my heart and was brought to tears. With each lesson learned, I grew more compassionate as a healer. There were days where I thought I should just quit, and others where my client had the AH-HA moment making me continue for just one more day. My experiences may not be what you experience. I want you to understand the many possibilities that can happen. Sometimes reading another's experiences makes it so much easier to keep going. That is my wish for you, keep going! Yes, the journey is hard, but I wouldn't have it any other way now.

THANK YOU!!

I want to whole heartedly THANK God, Jesus, Mary, Joseph, Anna, Dr. Usui, Mrs. Takata, Seraph Rose Aura, Archangel Michael, Archangel Raphael, Archangel Gabriel, Archangel Uriel, Saints, Zaque and animal guides, Mom and Dad's and those ancestors of the light for helping me from the spiritual realm. From the physical world, thank you to: Mom, Poopsie, Douglas, Brandon, Jill, Carrie, Jamie, Sierra, Denise, Suli, Len, Lee, Mara, Bryon, Leigh, Mary, Rita, Julie, Donna, Cindy, Kim, Brenda, Claire, Kathy, Keiko, Jennifer, Judy, all the fabulous clients and friends from A Hand in Healing and all the Reiki professionals who have helped blaze the path before me. Thank you all for the love and support given to me at one time or another. This book is dedicated to you who believed in me and Reiki and you who did not believe in Reiki. You all were instrumental in pushing me harder. You made me dig deeper into my beliefs to realize my soul purpose. I wouldn't have written this as quickly without my favorite stones, shells, incense, plants and trees helping me grow with nature's beauty every single day!

I am a skeptical person. If I have NOT experienced it, I don't believe it. Because of this, my experiences have been extraordinary. The non-believer in me constantly expects more. Each new experience deepens my understanding of Reiki and healing. The more Reiki I do, the more I notice increasing synchronicity. While reading a book or taking a class, the lesson from it appears in real life. I notice the lessons, and realize they happen to make me stop and listen. They happen to expand my heart, and fill me with my soul purpose. I noticed these experiences were not in any Reiki book, and I wanted to make this information available to others. This book is for you: the non-believer, the new Reiki Practitioner, the Reiki 2 Practitioner and the Reiki Master. It is filled with stories from my clients and my Reiki Master perspective. This is my journey, the perfecting of my Reiki destination. It is my hope that this book will give you the faith to keep going with your Reiki journey. I know that I will never be done learning, and each time I give Reiki to another person I learn something more and my belief in Reiki grows deeper. I wish that for everyone.

This book is set up from diaries I've kept for years, and the reflection of the occasions 16 years later. I found the title to the book before I understood that I needed to add the reflection part. Since then, it opened my eyes to a whole new world of memories. Some of the information is from experiences at A Hand in Healing, my wellness center. Many lessons were learned about energy from other classes besides Reiki. My spiritual growth there was amazing and happened in a short period of time. Every experience you have is important to your path in life; sometimes you just don't recognize it at the time. This is why I want to encourage you to write in a diary, it's important to go back and remember what happened as well as what was learned. Life is like that, experiences bring us more understanding and make us grow whether we realize it or not. This is true for Reiki or any other life experience you are on the road to discovering. This is the reason for being here: experiencing, reflecting, growing and loving every minute of it!

My first relaxation session happened with Usui Reiki at the age of 35. A friend gave me a session after she took her Reiki 1 Practitioner class and I was blown away that I could be so relaxed. At the time, stress was at a high point, so if this could help, I needed to know how to do it! I had no idea that this ancient healing technique would be the method to get me to understand my soul, and lead me on the spiritual journey of my lifetime. Before Reiki, I was a bundle of nerves all the time. I thought in order for my life to be perfect, I had to be perfect. Clean house, good job, everything neat and orderly. Now I can say I was a mess, but I don't think I had a clue back then. At that time I drank too much soda, was a nail bitter and stressed all the time. Fifteen years later, I drink a lot of water, no soda, eat healthy, paint my nails and can manage stress! I never would have guessed Reiki would totally change my life! We know Reiki is for the mental, emotional and physical body....but for me too?

March 14, 1998

This was the day that I took the first part of my Traditional Usui Reiki 1 Practitioner class. The drive to the class had me thinking about my life, and my connection to God. I wondered what my life was supposed to be about, and at the age of 35, married with two young children I knew there was more I needed to accomplish personally. I prayed to God, with all my heart, to show me a sign that he was with me and give me guidance. I decided on the way over that I would not choose where to sit for the attunements. I had an intuitive moment where I thought I would be first to be attuned. I was ok with that, as my anxiety was at a high! I wanted to get the attunements as fast as possible so I could relax. My plan was to wait until the other fourteen people who signed up for class to sit down, and I would take the last chair. The Reiki Master Teacher (RMT) told us that she would begin attunements on the left and work her way down the row. Of course, no one sat in the first chair. So, I hesitantly sat down and was first to be attuned. My heart was racing since I had no idea what to expect. The RMT told us how the attunements would happen, instructed us to relax, and close our eyes. The RMT was in front of me and put her hand up in front of my head. I instantly saw a bright white light enter the room, and I turned towards the kitchen and opened my eyes to see where it was coming from, and it was gone. I closed my eyes again and there it was again, brighter than any light I had ever seen! I decided to remain calm and enjoy this experience. I felt an extreme heat. I can't think of anything which I can even compare it to, because I have never been on the sun! My whole body was sweating and I now realize my decision to wear sweats and a turtle neck was bad! When the RMT slapped my left hand while putting the symbols in, I felt the sting of the slap and jumped out of my almost relaxed state. I felt the energy, as heat, go into my left hand, and travel up my arm, across my chest, down the other arm and in my back all at once. I had NEVER felt anything like this in my life, and now I was scared. What is happening to me? I never meditated before, and now I was sweating, and crying from the depth of my stomach. I didn't even understand why I was crying, but tears continued to pour out of me. The person I came with is sitting next to me, rubbing my back in an effort to comfort me. I didn't understand what happened. After everyone was attuned, we all sat in a circle and I was asked to use the talking stick first. I explained the light, the RMT asked what I thought it was, and I didn't know at that moment. The Reiki story she told didn't explain Dr. Usui seeing the light come to him, but once I read that story, I knew it was what I experienced as well! I asked God to show me he was with me during the ride here, and he couldn't have been brighter!

Reflection: This was the first time I felt God was giving ME a sign! Now my attention was super enhanced to signs everywhere! Tip: YOU HAVE TO ASK from your heart in order to receive. Once you ask, keep the questions in your mind while actively searching for and recognizing the signs received to interpret the answers.

The next step was to give Reiki to others in the class. I was intuitively called to sit at my classmates head. My hands were sweating as soon as I started working on him and I was getting scared as I didn't know what was happening. I tried to get the sweating under control by wiping them on my pants but it didn't help. I finally tuned into him by just looking at his face and got so emotional, started crying, got up and went to the bathroom. I went back to his feet and he asked who was at his head and then stopped. He said it was such a strong energy, and I verified it because of the intensity of the heat coming from my hands. I knew then that I had something, but had no idea what. I was too embarrassed to ask what was going on, and just did my best to get through the rest of the day without another melt down. I had two attunements this day, and two the next. This was the first time I have ever felt like I may be psychic, as the information I was getting on the man were not my own thoughts. I couldn't understand how Reiki would be giving me this information and I then concluded it was my imagination.

Before beginning a session, I was taught to do this:

I ground myself and connect to Mother Earth. I ask her to bring me unconditional loving Reiki energy through my feet to my heart. Then I ask for Reiki energy from the Heavens to come through my hands to my heart. And finally ask for Reiki energy from the Universe to come through my head to my heart. Later in life I added: Dear God, Dr. Usui and Mrs. Takata, Jesus, Mary, all my angels and saints, guides and any ancestors of unconditional love and light who can help heal my client, please come forward to help me heal _____ today. Then I ask God to send the clients guides, angels and deities for my clients healing for the highest and greatest good. I stand for a moment and feel the energy go through me before sending distance Reiki or giving Reiki to my client. Before placing my hands on the client I say: Please send the Reiki energy that I need to heal _____ today.

Thank you!

Reflection: Don't be afraid to ask questions when you experience something out of the ordinary! If I had asked, I may not have been so emotional, or, I would have understood what was going on. I understand now that when looking at the clients face, you see the true love God created right in front of you! The emotion of that understanding is what made me start crying. I am not sure that in my Reiki 1 class we were told what an "I AM" presence is, your higher self, but that is what I was connecting to with this fellow Reiki 1 Practitioner.

We were asked to bring an item to absorb the energy of the Reiki 1 Practitioner class and leave it on the altar overnight. I chose to leave a family heirloom, a ring given to my Mother for her 8th grade graduation.

My Aunt had my Grandmothers wedding ring (from 1910) flattened and engraved just for my Mom in 1938! Mom gave me this ring to wear at the age of sixteen, and I wore it daily. This was the first time in nineteen years that it was off my finger. That night, I woke suddenly with a stabbing pain in the finger where I normally wore it. At first I thought I must have slept on it funny, but it was clear, very quickly, that my Grandmother was in the room with me. There was a huge energy at the foot of the bed that went up to the ceiling, I couldn't see it, but I felt it hovering. Grandmother passed in 1932 at the age of 41, and I never got to meet her. I only have one picture of her, and because Grandmother died when Mom was just 11 years old, she didn't even have any stories to share with me. With my eyes closed I remember saying to her, "I am so sorry I never got to meet you." This was the first time I ever tried to "talk" to her, and she made it clear that she was my Reiki guide watching over me. The conversation was from my mind to hers, no words were spoken. I could not see her, but I could hear her in my mind from my heart. It was a direct mind to mind connection, like praying to someone but they are also answering you. I cried myself back to sleep, missing the love I never got to experience with her in person. It made me realize that even if we don't know our relatives, they know us! This was the first time, and just the beginning of my ability to be able to "communicate" with those who have passed. It is interesting to me that I didn't meditate or call out to her, but I knew her instantly when I woke and realized the pain in my finger was from the missing ring. Is it because I was open to receiving the message from her that she came? Will this happen again? I was intrigued and lost at the same time, and worse, I had no one to explain it to me. The next day, I told RM what happened and she said my third eye is opening. "Ah Ha" I thought, but really had no idea what she meant by third eye opening....was it closed before? How do I know if it's open now? What do I do or who do I see to open it? Do I open and close it at will? It was now clear that I will be learning more than I ever imagined! I thought Reiki was just about relaxation!

Reflection: I should have asked Grandmother more questions. The first time this happened to me I was so surprised; I didn't take a moment to just be in the love. Had I understood this could happen, I would have been prepared. Also this is my first time realizing material things, like this ring, has more energy and symbolism to it than I ever realized!

I wouldn't say "I am a religious person." I did go to a Catholic church as a young child, but never felt "connected to God." I tried to figure out why

I am the spiritual person I am, as I didn't get it from my parents or anyone around me. Slowly, I started noticing coincidences that made me wonder, could that be a sign I was looking for? I always believed in God, and knew I had his Spirit inside me, but this weekend affirmed all my thoughts about me and the fact that God loves me for ME. Not for what religion I belong to, but just because I am me! I know God was with me at this class, and I now believed in the power of ME. God gives us what we need, when we need it. I needed to "see" the bright light and feel his heart. You say these things in your mind, but when it happens it was nothing like I expected to feel. I have never felt such calm within me. I understood that all would be fine, even though I didn't know what "fine" meant to me. They say that first you learn that God is in a church, and that you pray to God. Then you learn he is part of you…I truly believed it now. I will soon learn that God works through me and to become enlightened, that God works as us, that we are not separate from God.

Reflection: Although I understood the words, it made no sense that I was not separate from God. This didn't sink in until years after my Reiki Master class. If you can understand this earlier, it will make your healings happen quicker. If you realize that God works through you and puts you in certain situations for good, your life is less stressful. I now had a new sense of grounding that I never had before this connection. I was centered and able to concentrate on one thing at a time, and with this greater new focus was able to move through my "to do" list quicker!

The day after Reiki 1 Practitioner weekend I was extremely energetic, exhausted the next day, and had a major detox the week after! I thought I had the flu, but of course, no one else in the family had it, or got it from me after. Reiki sure made a difference in my physical body! I now used Reiki before my menstrual cycle to relieve cramps, bloating and PMS. I lost weight, and suddenly wanted broccoli like it was going out of style! Before Reiki, I drank Pepsi at least three times a day, and ate red meat. After Reiki, I wanted water like it was the best beverage ever! I could no longer eat red meat, all I could envision was the poor animal, and I recognized that it made me feel heavy energetically. My stomach felt bloated, and I felt like I was moving slowly. Chocolate has always been a daily "need" and I have come to understand it was what I needed to remain grounded. As time goes by I now realize what is happening. My body needs to be able to vibrate at a higher frequency, and anything that is keeping me from doing this will be eliminated. Sometimes it takes years to figure out what that is, but as always, I get all that is needed in perfect Divine timing. My body and subconscious mind was responding to doing all the things I needed to be healthy. It allows me to give a higher vibrational Reiki session to whoever needs it.

Reflection: Use Reiki as frequently as possible after your first Reiki class. Use it on food, beverages, plants, pets, Mother Earth and anyone who will let you practice on them. If you make this a part of your daily ritual, change happens faster. Take time to give Reiki to your food and beverages before you eat. As you water plants give Reiki to them, or simply put Reiki in the water before you water them. Let the intention be for the highest and greatest good, and it will be. I always have chocolate that I have infused Reiki into available in my Reiki room. Many times after Reiki, clients are lightheaded and chocolate assists in grounding them quickly, especially with the added Reiki!

Years earlier, my adopted Grandmother passed before Easter. I had the privilege of knowing this amazing woman who was a foster Mother to several children. I remembered that she had given me the Miraculous Mary Medal years before and decided I needed to wear it now, especially when I needed patience. Grandma was the role model of patience and compassion, and I needed her message today. It becomes clear that Divine timing is making its way into my life, although I am not picking up on it yet. I begin to understand that crosses and medals are symbols which have their own power and why many people use them. This got me thinking more about getting the Reiki 2 Practitioner certification, since it uses symbols to increase the power of Reiki. I finally got to the point where I felt the Reiki I was getting wasn't enough, I needed more healing power.

April 16, 1999

I had my Reiki 2 Practitioner attunements, and needed a nap about 3 hours after class! That night, I felt tingling in my feet up my legs on both sides of each leg. Then my lower back hurt. Although red is my favorite color, I had no idea how much root chakra work I needed! We get what we need while giving Reiki to others, and I was slowly getting my intuition to work while giving Reiki to clients. I could feel my clients pain on my body exactly where they needed it on their body. By listening to my intuition, it guides me to give Reiki wherever my body feels pain. When I listen to it, and go to the spot, the pain instantly goes away. It seems especially strong with family members. In the months that follow, I am having a hard time going to places with a lot of people. The grocery store on a Saturday was difficult as I could feel pain from the fellow shoppers while waiting in line. I knew exactly where it was on them and would have to send Reiki with my eyes to help each person. I would then ask their guardian angels to stay with them and continue to heal and protect them. In subsequent years I would not go to the mall (especially at Christmas) as I would get a headache and stomachache from feeling all the fast moving energy there.

Daily Protection: I say this as a part of my morning routine before getting out of bed...

Ask God, and your Reiki Guides to send you unconditional loving light energy to your crown chakra. Wait until you feel it here, and then ask that it move to your third eye, and continue down to the root chakra and the earth chakra below your feet. Next, ask Mother Earth to bring energy up from the earth chakra to your root and see it continue to rise up to the crown chakra. Next, ask for a diamond netting to cover you, 360 degrees around you. This lets positive energy in and out but keeps negative energy out. Finally, invite St. Germaine to protect your entire body with his silver violet flame! Ask this energy to protect you for 24 hours. Thank YOU!

Reflection: I know many Reiki Practitioners who can't tolerate crowds. My advice is to protect yourself before you go into the building. I generally do this as I am walking from my car to the store, if it didn't occur to me before this point. Ask your guides to protect you from any negative people, places or things. Archangel Michael protects in a heartbeat, just ask! You can also shield yourself by imagining a layer of diamond netting totally covering your body, from head to toe. It will enhance the energy you send out as well as allow positive energy in. Once I started doing this, shopping was no longer an issue. Carrying black tourmaline in your pockets will help to keep you grounded as well as absorb negative energy before getting to you. I typically have one in each pocket so I can just reach in and hold it if necessary. If talking to someone I feel uncomfortable with, I will stand with my arms folded and legs crossed. The crossing protects from negative energy coming at me. I now make it a point to pray to God on a daily basis for protection from any negative energy from anyone. If you make this a part of your routine, there is no way for others to be able to change your energy without your verbal permission.

Reflection: I use the Reiki symbols where ever I am to establish a "safe zone" around me. First, I focus on protecting the building, then on protecting the people inside. I notice people who seem to be having physical issues and send them Reiki individually as well as to the group as a whole. At the gym, I send Reiki to the building before getting out of the car. Once inside, I use the symbols on the walls, ceiling and floor to protect and heal everyone within. As I am on the treadmill, I send the symbols to the treadmill so I become one with it and we are working together for my highest and greatest good. I ask Jesus to sit in the back of my heart chakra and heal every atom, cell, fiber, tissue, nerve, muscle, organ and skin. I keep my focus on my body and notice what is hurting. I ask Jesus to go to the spot and heal it now. It is done instantly! I have aerobic music on in the background to keep me moving to a higher vibration. Once I am in a healing zone, I move effortlessly to the music and there is no pain in my body. In this healing zone, I ask God to bring me more strength, more balance and more oneness. When I leave, I feel blessed for the time to bring my physical body more of what it needs to keep my spirit moving forward as well.

August 1999

I assist during Reiki Practitioner class. My concern was that I really had nothing to offer at this class. That quickly went away once I worked on our first Practitioner. Everyone felt done and removed their hands and that intensified my feelings of tingling, shaking and such intense pain that I was crying. It lasted at least ten minutes before I could end the session. I was removing the negative energy to Mother Earth to recycle to love. I asked her what she felt, and she said her family member who she had not seen in a long time who had died from cancer was with her. A lot of pain was in that relationship and she thanked me with a hug and said she needed to let it go. The client had a lot of feelings inside, and was grateful she was able to get those feelings out, for fear they would turn into disease. This is about the time I started reading Caroline Myss's book: Anatomy of the Spirit, The Seven Stages of Power and Healing. I practically memorized Part II, The Seven Sacred Truths "that lists issues and illnesses that can serve as a major influence in the development of any of the noted dysfunctions in each of the specified chakra descriptions." As I reviewed the lists, I thought of people I knew with issues and looked up the emotion that was the cause. To my amazement, it was correct every time! This will prove to me over and over in every session that emotions are to be taken seriously, explored and healed to remain healthy.

The next Reiki 1 Practitioner I work on is female, and I listen to my intuition, angels and guides as they tell me to go to her thighs, then legs. Within minutes I moved to the right leg and the heat intensified. We worked on her together for a while before I was left alone to finish. Again I felt intense heat, my hands were shaking and sweating, and my heart was racing. I knew that once I connect with the person's energy I am feeling their emotions and physical symptoms. When you first feel these things, you believe something is wrong with you; but it really is God working through you to heal your client. It's hard, at first, to stay with these feelings as they are intense and you want to stop. That's when I learned to ask for only the information I need to heal them, so as to not take on any additional pain that I can't physically handle, and be able to remain professional. I felt heavy pressure and kept getting a message, "this is so hard." After we stopped, I asked if she had arthritis in her right leg. She said "yes, from an old high school injury." Then I asked if there was something going on in her life that was hard. "Yes, I have a son who is dying." My eyes filled with tears as she admitted that the pain was so hard, that she couldn't even cry. WOW! That was exactly what I was feeling. I now understood my ability and needed to figure out the best way to help people deal with their emotions. It is quite unsettling to feel these things and wonder if they are true. I found that I needed to question my guides three times to get a yes answer from them in order to trust the information I am given. Only then do I bring up the topic with the client and it's always correct. Trusting your intuition is difficult, but having Reiki guides to validate the answers helps. The more your client validates, the easier it gets.

Reflection: Trusting your intuition should be taught in every Reiki 1 class. My fears would not have existed had I understood this very important piece of communication with Reiki. There is a difference between your intuition telling you something and you thinking it. Intuition says "you" but you say "I".

Another client has extremely heavy energy in his arms. I kept thinking this slender man has such a load on his arms. I kept questioning it and finally came to the conclusion that there was a heavy message he had to communicate, but was holding back. I asked the guides three times, and was told to advise him to say the message he had needed to communicate. He broke down in tears saying that he needed to discuss a difficult topic with his parents and I gave him the confidence to go ahead and tell them he is homosexual. My information was confirmation that he is strong enough to do it. Sometimes you don't get all the information, but just enough to verify for the client what they are thinking is truly what they need to do.

Reflection: This is very hard to do, but I found if the information needs to be said, it won't leave me alone. It keeps playing over and over in my head until I say it. This sometimes happens so I can formulate a better way to give the information so I don't hurt the person's feelings. Reiki is love, so any message that needs to be said must be given in the most loving way possible. I simply converse about it in my head until I have the correct words to say with a loving intention.

September 1999

A friend asked me to send distance Reiki to her family member who has a brain tumor. I don't know anything more than this info and find it challenging to see what I can interpret. The first time I send Reiki I feel how tired she is and that Reiki is needed on the right side. The second time I send Reiki, I have a conversation with her "I AM" presence, her soul. I mention that medicine is not the only solution. God is the true healer, and she seems skeptical, shrugging her shoulders. This is not something I see, it's a feeling. I am learning to trust these feelings. I talked to her about being able to ride a bike and go for a walk or the beach to pick up seashells; she liked that idea as I feel a smile. Then we discussed children and the miracle of life. Even if she couldn't have children of her own, the possibility of adopting children is still an option. What a wonder gift that is to both the parents and child. I was not sure that I made any progress today, she is exhausted, and there is a feeling of such tiredness.

I take notes of all of this to tell my clients family member who I had not talked about these first two distance sessions yet. I sent her an email and told her it was around 3:30pm Monday when I sent the Reiki. The family member found out that is when she woke up from surgery. I had goosebumps! I also told her that the client was very, very tired and I asked her to talk to God. She really had given up and I'm trying hard to get her to stay with us. I realize that this is her choice; I just want to be sure that she thinks of all the options. The big hug and thank you from the family member was enough to know that somehow this little bit of information was encouraging to her.

Wednesday's distance Reiki session was between 11:00-11:30pm, I got a strong reaction when I asked if she spoke with God. I sent Reiki from her feet through her whole body to her head. I gave her Reiki on her head for a long time, she was dizzy for a while and I explained it's because the equilibrium was coming back and trying to rebalance her. (I am not a doctor, nor would I be able to understand this, I trust this information is coming from a higher source.) I asked that the Angel of Hope stay with her. I asked that anytime she doubted anything, to remember God's love and energy. He is always there to protect and guide her. I gave her a hug and she didn't want to go. I told her it's important that she rest. She was energized, but I was exhausted!

I sent Reiki again Thursday 8:30 am, she is still very tired. I explained I would stay with her, and send more energy later. I asked if she had made contact with her mom yet, she said no. (I feel this as a head shaking back and forth) I told her she should let her Mom know she is ok and hopeful. The energy was not as strong going to her today. I take that as a good sign that she doesn't need as much.

3:30pm Friday afternoon, she has much better energy today! She spoke with her Mom and has much more energy for a longer period of time. She's no longer giving up! She's fighting and strong!

8:30-9:45 am Sunday I Reiki her right ear, I felt an object in her ear, I could not tell if it was a round or square metal piece, but I knew it should not be there, and I took it out. The heat intensified and I stayed with it until my hands returned to a normal temperature.

8:30am Monday she's very weak, still hesitant about why she is here, I asked her to talk to God any time; he is ALWAYS there for you. I explained Reiki more, that only unconditional loving energy from GOD comes to you for your highest and greatest good. God is the one who decides when you go, not you. I asked her to think about what she accomplished if the plan is leaving now. Does she understand that this may come back again if she doesn't heal it this lifetime? There is a reason this is here now, you can heal it!

8:30-9:15 am Tuesday I sent Reiki to the top of her head, her ear is burning up, with pain on top of her head. I released the ear issue by telling it that it was no longer needed here, it was time to go, thanks for the lesson,

I love you. I explained to her that she must deal with the problem to get rid of it. You don't want to continuously carry it around; she shakes her head in agreement. She said it may be too painful to deal with, and I advised God wouldn't give her anything she could not handle. She is now thinking she could be a role model for those like her in the future who need help. She understands it all, and has been there!

2:00-2:15 Wednesday, she's out of the woods! She's going to be fine! Her birthday is Saturday and she wants chocolate cake and French vanilla frosting. Her health is most important now; I cried happy tears for her. Her energy is up and I didn't get intense energy feelings in her head. I know she is going to be well; this is the best birthday ever!

In December her family member told me they all gathered for the holiday, the Dr. did have to insert a metal tube into her ear to release fluid. I got goosebumps when I found out it's the right ear! So the information I am getting is correct! This is unbelievable to me, that I know this information, and can use it to help someone. My tears of joy are from God's guidance, and I am so grateful.

Reflection: I didn't realize that listening or trusting your feelings is a psychic gift! I assumed this is how all Reiki Practitioners received distance healing information. It's not until I began teaching it that I realize this is not as common. Reiki opens your intuition and brings you to an understanding of your gifts. Clairvoyance is being able to see images, clairaudience is being able to hear messages through thoughts, clairsentience is being able to feel emotions and feelings of others and claircognizance is having clear knowing. I believe that I was always able to feel emotions at an early age. I remember being afraid of certain people and staying away from them. Then the knowing developed from the feelings. I would feel something and just know what to do because of it. My hearing developed only with my distance Reiki but I don't see images much at all, yet.

During distant Reiki sessions, I get feelings on my hand where I imagine them lying down with their head to the tips of my fingers. The third eye chakra is in the section of the finger where the fingertip bends to the knuckle. The throat chakra is from the knuckle to where the finger joins the hand. The heart chakra is almost in the middle of the hand, solar plexus just below that, sacral under solar and root where the hand meets the wrist. I may feel a lot of energy at the crown chakra, and ask the guides if they are with us. This is a combination of feeling, hearing, and knowing how to continue. Once they begin chatting through me, my guides and the person's guides and I AM presence do the work. The questions flow through my mind to ask the person to help guide them through the process. A big part of it is patience to just let the session unfold. When I first began, I didn't always know when I was finished. This takes time to practice and understand within you.

Two days before the next Reiki 1 class I thought, I need new sneakers. And wouldn't you know it; Reiki class was about standing up for yourself. One of the clients came in and told us that she was making a huge career change, and she looked alive with passion now! Client two took the class and also needed to stand up for herself, after years of marriage and separation, she's decided to get a divorce but doesn't want to hurt her husband. We all agreed to give her the strength she needs to make a decision. Her legs needed Reiki and she had a spot in her back where she feels like someone is stabbing her in the back. Her friend came and we helped put the strength back into her legs. There was a lot of pent up anxiety about her children. It was as if we performed a way to let this out, she cried, shook and after was visibly calm. All three were so glad they came, it was amazing to me. It wasn't until the next day that I realized my feet still hurt and I needed to learn to stand up for myself as well. I am finally realizing my abilities, and when I finally acknowledged my gift, the pain in my feet vanished, without new shoes. When I understood the symbolism of the sneakers in my mind, then the message of being able to stand up for yourself emerged! This was the first time that I would realize that about 2-3 days before my classes, a general theme would show up. I would always know before the class what the client was feeling and get a clear picture of what would be needed for stones, which chakra's would need most help and figure out which colors to wear for the class. This information would come while alone, randomly, in the shower or car driving to work. I never had to ask, it would just come. The energy knows I need this info and it appears.

Reflection: This continues to happen for me all the time; it is the way it works, my process so to speak. Whatever your process is, notice it, and be one with it. Several times I have doubted what I need to wear and always end up changing to put on what I was originally told. Now I just do it the first time!

Every day, when I wake up, I think about what plans I have for the day. Am I giving Reiki, am I teaching Reiki? If I am giving Reiki, do I have an understanding of what it is that is needed? I meditate on it for a few minutes and ask my stone collection which ones I need to work with that day. They tell me and if I am in doubt, I ask three times and decide from that answer. I get stones to work with and colors to wear that are exactly what is needed to the Practitioners in the class. This progressed to also every day of the week, whether or not I am giving Reiki. I cannot just get dressed by randomly picking something from the closet. If I just need more energy, my "GO TO" colors are red, black and white. Everyone has their own colors that just make them feel energized! Figure out those colors and have them ready! There are days I get dressed three times before I feel like its "right". I do the same thing with jewelry, and sometimes I need certain jewelry and then the outfit follows. Intuition is important here, and when I pay attention to it on a daily basis, my getting dressed plan goes much smoother. One main factor is pockets. I need pants with pockets or a jacket with them to carry all the stones with me. I tend to wear multiple necklaces for the stones that are needed energetically. Due to the energy needed, the whole outfit and jewelry tends to coordinate well.

My wardrobe has all the chakra colors in it, and I suggest anyone in this field also own at least one shirt of every chakra color. There are different chakra color charts, and which ever one you are comfortable with is the one you should use! People say different things about every color. I LOVE the color red, however others see it as a warning color. Wear what makes you happy, and don't worry about anyone else's opinion! Buy clothing in colors that are bright and crisp, pastels of the colors work, but not as quickly. Remember, when you're trying to get the chakras to vibrate at a higher frequency, color matters. Stay away from what I call the "fall" colors....maroon, for example, doesn't have the same power as fire engine red. For this reason alone, I sometimes wish I lived in a warmer climate where "fall" colors almost don't exist. I don't have gray tops, as it is too dreary and makes me feel down. I do have black tops but wear them infrequently. White is a great color but hard to find in nice winter weight pants, so I typically only wear that in spring through fall here in New England. If you can't wear a certain color during the day, at least sleep in it at night. Not many people like the colors orange and yellow, so if this is an issue, wear it as underwear, socks or sleepwear. Also consider buying sheets in the color you do not like. Once your body gets used to the energy of it, you will want to wear it as a shirt color. If yellow is your issue, consider wearing more gold jewelry instead. Consider where the color is in the chakras as well....do you own a pair of red jeans? Dressing in the color in the right location is an added plus! Working with Reiki and color, we use matching stones for the chakras. If someone is having a root chakra issue, I would recommend red jeans, underwear, socks, boots or shoes along with carrying stones like red jasper, garnet and ruby jewelry. Then add more red to the diet: cranberry or tomato juice, spaghetti sauce, beets, radishes, apples, strawberries, etc. These changes to add a specific color to your physical world will do wonders to get you to think more about your red chakra issue. When you put more emphasis on healing something, your focus shifts and the answer is likely to come to you quicker.

There are times when I need to wear a specific piece of jewelry for the metaphysical properties and that alone will determine what I wear for clothing. I just stand in front of the jewelry armoire and ask which piece needs to work with me today, and the right piece just jumps out at me. Try to listen to what is being told to you; once you do it will happen again and again!

March 12, 2000

I send distance Reiki to a male client, I found he's hanging onto what looks like an old shriveled up head. I asked him who it was, he replied, "me, after love." He really thinks he lost himself once his wife entered the picture. He honestly thinks that he needs to work to provide his wife with everything she wants financially. He said "I need to provide money for her to spend." I said: "Then you need to know her better so you can see she's not like that." "How?" he asked. "Talk to her," I told him. He needs to spend more time understanding this part of his wife. He had no more to say. Hopefully this will sink in and help their relationship. Down the road, the stress of working takes a toll on him. He had three minor car accidents, before a car accident that totaled his car. He was lucky to be alive. This is what saved his life. He couldn't continue to live like he was and had no idea how to confront his wife. The car accident changed their communication. Communication is important in every relationship. If you can't talk about it, you can't begin to fix it.

Reflection: The image I saw during distance Reiki of the shriveled up head was a metaphor of him resisting the flow of life. The accident forced them to discuss issues. Don't wait until you get to the breaking point, work on it as it appears each day. Life is difficult and full of obstacles that are trying to prevent you from becoming the greatest version of yourself. If you don't deal with it as it appears, it tends to get worse so you have no other choice but to deal with it.

August 20, 2000

I felt four wings sprout from my spine while in the shower today. I asked Archangel Gabriel why I didn't feel like an angel, "you will" was the response. This feeling stayed with me as I exited the shower and I turned sideways to be sure they fit through the door! I looked in the mirror, and of course I could not see them. I am so amazed that I felt them! I am so blessed! I thanked God for giving me the ability to help heal others. It's in my soul, and I feel grateful in every cell of my being. I am noticing more connections to the angels in everyday life. I am grateful to my information angel who is with me every time I visit the library. Every time I need something, the book is there falling into my hands at the right time. I realize later this is Gabriel, the angel of communication helping me!

Looking back over my lifetime, I can say I've had an angel with me every step of the way. Everyone knows they have a guardian angel with them since birth. I always wondered who mine is as I have always conversed with her in my head. If there was something I wanted, I became obsessed with praying about it. "God, please help me find_____" and sure enough, it would happen. Of course these were things for my highest and greatest good, or they would not have happened. Finding the perfect husband, and jobs I have enjoyed, all happened at the perfect time. I remember when I noticed this gift. I wanted a red Camry. I looked it up, and I knew the bells and whistles I wanted in the car. I prayed about it and waited. I asked to be shown the right place and time to find it. Then one day, I felt an urgency to go to a certain dealership, as I knew it was there, waiting for me. When the salesman approached, I told him: "I am here to make your job easy today. I am looking for a used red Camry. It has airbags in front and sides." He said "one just came in yesterday" and I purchased it within two hours. Before Reiki my intuition was not as open, but now the clarity is amazing!

Reflection: I used to think I had intuition, and knew to listen to my gut instinct. Once your angels are having conversations with you, and you begin following the instructions, situations that may have taken longer to complete in the past are now quick! My son had an experience while on vacation with a group of people. They were all to go together in one car and suddenly he had to get out of the car before leaving. He said his stomach wasn't right and he just apologized and got out of the car. When they returned, the car had been in an accident, and got hit right where he would have been sitting. He just listened to the intuition without really knowing why. This is how it starts with many people; something just makes you instinctively do something at the spur of the moment. I explained to him, "that is your intuition working with you. Be grateful to your guides for helping you, just say thank you as an acknowledgement that they are working with you and they will continue to help you." If you have a relative with intuitive ability, talk to them about how they recognized it. The conversation will help you understand more about your connection as well!

The last Reiki 2 Practitioner class of the year 2000 had 3 clients and was very powerful. This 2 day class was broken up into two months. In August we did attunements and gave private sessions to client one who is put together emotionally, but just needed some back work from a recent car accident. Client 2 was a different story; most of her issues were in a rib that was sticking out at the time. We helped her understand issues she had with her father and were trying really hard to "breakthrough" a point in her back that I just felt stuck in energetically. Client 3 understood Reiki but just wasn't convinced of the true miracles it can perform. He didn't say this, but I could tell from conversations about it. Later, we had a huge conversation about gardening. Client 3 "told" the fairies what he wanted and then was disappointed when he didn't get what he expected. When I asked what his part of the deal was, he said, "I told them." I said: "that's the problem, you TOLD them. You didn't ask, or say thank you. You TOLD them." "OH, I see," he said. I responded, "You can't expect them to help you if your intent isn't there. You had no intentions to help or praise them, why would they help you?" I started to see a light bulb go on, but knew there was more to come. We had a long conversation about intent and faith. "You can't do something once and think it will be done. This new thought pattern must become a part of who you are and what you do, in order for the results to manifest." It was interesting that these words were not mine. I didn't think about the conversation, it was as if the answers just flowed through me. I didn't think of it at the time, but is this Gabriel helping again? They left to return the following week for part 2 of class.

Reflection: Medical Clairvoyant Edgar Cayce used to say "the mind is the builder" and I understand this now. Your thoughts either help you get what you need to move forward or prevent it from happening. Watch your thoughts, words and deeds. Every one of them matters. You must keep your thoughts positive, as any negativity will bring down all the good that you have worked to increase.

Three days before they were returning for the next Reiki class I started getting energy. Normally, I need to ask for it, this day I felt it without asking. When Client 3 arrived, I told him it was going to be a tough day for him. Client 2 asked if we were going to work on him, of course, I was dying to work on him! My plan was to start at his heart and he would instantly cry. WRONG. I started at his heart, Client 2 worked at his stomach, Client 1 at his feet and another at his neck. I stood there for a while and felt nothing. Then I thought this is going to take longer than I thought. A few more minutes and Client 1 said she felt unbalanced like the right side was more balanced than the left. I was on the left and knew that's why I was here. Client 2 felt nothing in the stomach and I asked her to put her hands on top of mine at the heart chakra. I asked Client 3 what he was feeling in his heart. He didn't say anything. I told him I felt anger and that he needed to let go of it. I am crying now. I asked him to put his anger in his left hand, a few minutes pass, and then I told him to dump it into Mother Earth and ask her to recycle it to love, and thank her. Next, we replaced the anger with love. He felt better and I asked him to let go of all the past hurts in his life. We had lunch and then went to another location for meditation. He was traveling with me, and we had a long talk about his anger. He was upset with family. He felt guilty that he didn't get to spend time with his mom. He was angry with his ex-wife for being dishonest about their relationship to their children. I told him he needed to send Reiki to the children so they would come back to him. He wasn't sure he wanted them back. I asked him, "What kind of changes would they have to make in their hearts in order to knock on your door?" Then the light bulb moment came. He said, "I never thought about it that way." I asked "Don't you want a chance to start again? Don't you want them to come in?" "Yep," he said with a choked up voice. I said "Okay then. Be open to them, allow the option." By the end of the conversation, he was thinking in a new way. I was thrilled to be a part of that, although I couldn't take credit for the words that came out of my mouth. I was given that information to say; I didn't think of it, it just flowed through me, God and the angels knew how to get Client 3's attention.

Reflection: All these emotions Client 3 was holding on to are related to love, which is what I felt before he arrived. The emotions I am witnessing do manifest in the organ that it is related to, confirming Caroline Myss' work! Over and over, I will be given clients to reinforce this truth. There will be those who go to a doctor, chiropractor, or physical therapist and still have no results because they don't get to the core emotion of the issue.

This is what I want to do in my life! It's difficult work getting through the pain of the past. It's hard to feel old emotions and think in a different way in order to release it. But once you are on the other side of pain, the intense freedom from holding onto it is amazing! I prayed to God to let me be a Reiki healer, to see angels and let me help people on their paths. I was told "no", that my job would be a soul healer. It made sense after the conversation with Client 3. I told a friend I was concerned as there are no books on soul healing. I don't like the sound of "Soul Healing" as if there is something "wrong" with a person's soul. I look to God to provide the people who need healing and the method on how to heal it. God is leading me down this path. I've been picking up different things since starting Reiki a few years ago. Emotions are always strong with my clients and I'm always right about which emotion, I just don't have all the info to back up the emotion. I knew Client 3 was angry, but not why. Maybe I'll be able to get more information soon. Or maybe I don't need to know; maybe this is where the client input is important. I've been blessed by God to be able to help people get past their issues and move on. I trust God to bring me where I need to go.

This "soul healing or soul developing" started a huge conversation with a friend. She didn't want me or anyone else to change her soul; she said that is for her alone to decide. I started with the obvious, "Isn't that what Reiki Practitioners do on a daily basis? The client has free will and this is why when sending distance Reiki, your client may or may not heal. The soul is still in charge of deciding. The soul considers all ideas that come to it, decides if that is true for it and then it influences the person one way or the other." She said, "That is on a verbal knowing, not subconscious." I argued, "Distance Reiki is subconscious healing. You get permission from the client to give distance Reiki for their highest and greatest good." If that is not what you want then you would not give permission for it. It is my belief that we all want to "re-create yourself anew in the next grandest version of the greatest vision ever you held about Who You Are" as my favorite author Donald Neal Walsh, writer of <u>Conversations with God</u> would say. Sometimes the beliefs we have need to be challenged in order for the best to happen. This is why, in my opinion, "bad" things happen. They make you to step back and re-evaluate what is going on in your life. Sometimes you are redirected on a totally different path than you would have ever taken alone. Is this God helping you to find your soul? This may be the soul path that you were meant to be on all along. Our conversation did more to cause a rift in our relationship than anything we had previously discussed. I can't believe that anything but good can come from Reiki, as it cannot be used for harm. William Lee Rand wrote this from Dr. Usui in The History of Reiki:

"The phase of life is very changeable in these days, and people's thoughts are apt to change, too. Could we fortunately succeed in spreading the REIKI cure everywhere, we feel sure that it would have to be very helpful in order to prevent people from disordering their moral sense. It never extends people anything but the benefits of healing long term illness, chronic disease and bad habit."

Reflection: Years later, a Reiki 1 Practitioner talked about when she went to McDonald's to get a bacon cheeseburger. She was shocked when she got to the drive-thru and ordered a salad. She said she actually spun around to see who said that, as her thoughts were not on a salad. She asked me what happened. I told her once you take Reiki; your subconscious mind knows what it needs to be healthy. Clearly it was not a bacon cheeseburger.

March 2001

A client who had a heavy left shoulder comes for a Reiki session. The left side is the feminine side, and trusting what she is receiving for information is correct for her. I said it feels like: "the entire world is on your shoulders, everything is up to you." She said: "I feel responsible for everything in my family." She said her husband is into work aka "the provider" and she handles all the family stuff. Since he is not an emotional person, she tries not to be emotional. She said "I need to feel inner peace and I only feel that when I go to school or am pregnant." I told her, "That's not a good reason to do either; soon you'll be left with this feeling again." To balance this feeling, she needed to feel a belief in her own power to provide. In a sense, she has shut down that part of her life. Everyone needs to be able to share emotions with their partners and this client has not figured this out yet. I didn't tell her but losing her power to her husband would bring on more issues than not dealing with it. In months to come, she started having migraines. We know from the crown chakra, overthinking everything versus just talking about it can lead to migraines. Her migraines brought on lost work days, and began affecting family outings. This was her way of getting the inner peace that she couldn't get any other way.

Reflection: Your body gets what it needs every time. Once you figure out why it's happening you are now responsible to decide if you can make a change to heal it. If you think the change is too hard, the symptom will not only stay with you, but possibly get worse. In order to heal any chronic condition, your mind has to want it to change, and you allow the healing. There have been people who would rather hold onto the condition than heal. That is their choice. It is very difficult as a Reiki Master to know how the person could heal, but not be able to convince them it is possible.

May 20, 2001

I FINALLY convinced a friend to take Reiki! I've known for years that she's needed this but the timing wasn't right before now. I was so impatient! I wanted her to take it so bad, as I knew it would help with her medical issues. She had always given me excuses of why she couldn't come. When I finally told her to come for half a day, she decided to do it. She finally released her guilt about her last encounter with her sister before her sister died. When class was over, she left a new woman! She had more energy than she ever had, and quickly changed a lot of things in her life. I am so impressed! I wished she had done it sooner! People she's known for a long time tell her she looks younger, and it wasn't even a week since she did it! She used Reiki on herself for 3 hours a day at times, for several medical issues and is so grateful to be able to heal herself! In June my friend and I discover the power of stones and crystals with Reiki! We each have our special rocks we keep with us daily. We looked up the stones we needed based on our given names at birth, from author Melody's book: Love is in the Earth. Each letter of your name has a vibration, and each stone has been given a number that goes with that vibration. When you determine what numbers are missing from your name, and add those stones to your daily work, it's amazing the energy you get to make you complete. We now see a difference in relationships of the people who came for Reiki classes who are using a combination of Reiki and stones. Everyone is calmer, more peaceful! It's an awesome sight to sit back and watch as they realize God and Universal Energy is so powerful and is what they're missing. They are noticing small differences on a daily basis that are making a big impact on their lives. Months later, my friend is more engaged with her work and her business is booming!

Reflection: By healing the physical body, Reiki brings the joy of life back. Some doctors treat physical injuries. When you see them, they rarely dig deep into your personal life story to see a complete picture. Other doctors treat mental illness but don't add anything spiritual. Reiki involves the mind, body and spirit. We are not licensed doctors and do not replace their services; however, I know the complementary healing that Reiki provides. This is the first time I witness this change of spirit, and am in awe!

June 2001

I haven't made much money at Reiki, yet I know the major changes that it has made in the lives I've touched have made it worth more than any amount of money I could have charged. I have watched people have the AH-HA moment more often than I ever thought possible, and that in itself is a gift of a life time. I don't understand why more people aren't using Reiki. I feel like yelling from a mountain top, "TRY REIKI!" I notice this seems to be the "last resort" for many people, and I wish it was at the top of their list instead of the bottom!

I connected with one of my Guardian angels, her name is Rawish. I am grateful to know her name now! I look up the name and find it means: track, "the permanent way." I know Reiki will be the permanent way of life for me, so this rings true! As I know she helps me with finding me a parking spot near the front of any parking area I am in. I just ask her for help as I am driving into the lot, and listen. She tells me where to turn and she's always right! This is so exciting, I am humbled! My family laughs when they are with me, as they just think it's a coincidence.

Reflection: My son tries out this theory at a mall during the Christmas shopping season. He not only gets a front row parking spot, but also found a twenty dollar bill on the ground when opening the car door. Now he is a believer! I really do believe experiencing something is the way to understanding!

July 2001

I practiced attunements on another client today. I felt intense heat in his left hand and also in his feet as I tried to ground him. I also felt a lot of heat in his crown chakra. We had a conversation about why I am teaching people how to heal themselves versus just charging for Reiki sessions. I explained "I am changing the way people heal themselves and their families. Physically, emotionally and sometimes spiritually, a more intense and a deeper healing occur with Reiki. I can help heal by teaching others to pass it on. On Earth as it is in Heaven, I believe this is what God means. We can all be healed with Reiki! " He said "that's ridiculous, then if everyone is healed, then what?" I said, "This has been around since the 1600's, maybe forever in different names or intensities. Wouldn't it be nice to live in heaven?" He couldn't perceive it. But, I got a new thought process into his mind. I planted the seeds of love, respect and honor. In August I asked him if he's been doing Reiki, he said "yes", I asked "where?", and he pointed to his heart! He asked me what he should be thinking or asking, I told him to ask for unconditional loving healing, and think with his heart, not his head. Any time you give Reiki attunements to people, it triggers physical changes. It makes the client re-evaluate their entire life: job, relationships and their purpose in life. This is something that takes years for my self-confidence to trust.

Reflection: it is so hard to explain Reiki to people. It's almost like the word healing is overused in today's society. When I tell people, if you believe it, it will heal you, they look at me like I am just using flowery words. This started as a "good friend" helping me out as a client. He never expected it to actually be effective on him. I love the "AH-HA" moments when the clients realize it really is doing something!

August 18, 2001

A client asked me to clear her and her house of spirit attachments. She felt the presence of "Mr. Smith" in the hallway of her house. He had passed in the house over 20 years ago. The night before I had her prepare a water blessing for the house containing lavender for healing, basil and rosemary for clarity and lemon juice for cleansing. We both infused Reiki into the water as well, for the highest and greatest good of all. We lit sage and a white candle to escort Mr. Smith to a place of unconditional love. We started by smudging each other with sage before clearing the entity from the house. We started on the lowest level and worked our way to the top floor; starting in the East, South, West and North on each floor before going to the next floor. We repeated these prayers from Denise Linn's book: Sacred Space, throughout the entire clearing:

"God may my prayers travel up this smoke to you, that you may bring blessings and peace to this room and all who occupy it now or in the future. I know that your blessings travel down through this smoke to us and we give thanks for all blessings received."

Then I asked for protection for me and any other living, breathing being, even though I asked for protection before I even arrived. Next, I asked for our angels and guides and any other energy of unconditional love who wanted to help clear the house to come forward. I said "I speak on behalf of my friend and with the protection of Jesus Christ. I demand that any and all spirit attachments leave my friend's energy now. I bind your energy to you in the name of Jesus Christ. (I used Jesus at her request, but you can use any deity you are comfortable with) I ask the angels to escort this being back to a place of unconditional love and I forbid you to come back and attach again forever! We thank the angels for their guidance and love. May peace be with you on your journey!" Then I cleared my client with smudge again.

Next, I used my crystal bell and cleared the room. As we went along we found a spot in her living room that sounded different. The bell has a certain clear ring when the energy is fine, but now sounded off pitch. It was in this spot that my friend always saw Mr. Smith. We smudged it and used Cho Ku Rei's (CKR) several times. When we were done, the bell rang clear. The cellar felt the worst, over her major work area, it sounded like a thud. Again, we applied Reiki and I asked that all the negative energies come to me into my hands to recycle to Mother Earth as love. It felt very heavy, like a concrete block. I threw it into the core of the earth. I did all the walls and floor of the cellar. As I would go through clearing each space with the bell and Reiki, my friend would use the water to put a cross over each door and window for protection. She would say the following from Denise Linn's Sacred Space book as she did so:

"May this water be filled with spirit and may this room be cleansed and cleared by the power of water. As water renews and heals, may this room be renewed and healed by the grace of God. Amen."

When we were done, we said this closing prayer also from Denis Linn's Sacred Space book:

"May the God the creator that dwells in all things come forward and fill this home with blessings and protection. May this house be a loving home for all who enter. We ask that good thoughts and good actions emanate from this house. May this house bring comfort and healing for all who live here. May this house be a healing center of light, peace and love. I ask this in the name of God." Thank you, Amen.

My client felt a lighter energy in the house, sweetness in the air. That night they all slept soundly, as if at total peace and comfort. She said she could breathe deeply, something she could not do the past 23 years!

Reflection: We didn't sage ourselves again once this was complete, however we should have done so. Be sure to clear your chakras any time you do a clearing of this magnitude. I use rock salt in the shower and use the counterclockwise CKR symbol to open the chakras from the crown down to the root. I then ask Saint Germaine to come with his violet flame to clear any negative energy from any people, places or things I may have accumulated during the day. Once that is done, I sense the negative energy go down the drain and ask for positive energy to fill my chakra's back up while using the clockwise CKR from the root up to the crown. This should be done daily as part of your chakra shower routine!

September 11, 2001

The day America needs help. I was sleeping when my 79 year old mother knocked on my bedroom door telling me I needed to get up. "Why? Are you ok?" I asked. "Yes, you need to see the tv, a plane flew into the World Trade Center building in New York." We hurried to the TV, and as I watched, I instantly knew it was Osama Bin Laden's plot. I sat there and decided to send him distance Reiki. I asked for protection and although scared, I felt compelled to understand. I tried to send him LOVE, as it was clear he needed it. He didn't understand love. He said "power is more important." I asked him about his God and freedom of choice came up, God gave him that to do what he wants. But, I explained, "you're not allowing the innocent people a choice as to whether they want to die." He did not understand, he just didn't get it. Now, I am VERY scared! This is the first time I sent Reiki to someone who didn't understand that love and free will is for everyone, and you are not supposed to infringe on any one's free will. I decided to send love to him and whoever is closest to him to try and get him to understand the difference. Then I thought, am I infringing on his free will? Am I trying to change his free will? Yes, I am, for the sake of love, for the highest and greatest good of all. IF I were doing this for ANY other reason, it would not work. The Reiki would not get to him, or would simply be rejected by his I AM presence. I asked that if he rejects it that it goes to whoever is closest to him. Reiki never interferes with free will, but I am hoping that sending love will eventually shift his negative energy. I didn't send him any more after this day, and instead concentrated on the heroes of 9/11.

There was a two week period of time after that where I could not send Reiki, or get Reiki for even myself. At extreme times like these, I believe the energy is redirected to those who needed it most. The firemen, police officers, clergy, those lost and their families all were getting what they needed, with or without my Reiki. Prayers were being sent from every country on Earth, and although we were all shaken by this experience, it made us stronger. September 20, I was so extremely sad, at this point we heard over 5,422 people had lost their lives. Relatives had posted pictures of loved ones missing on buildings, memorials and news trucks. I spent days watching every TV show with a new story on a loved one who passed. Jeremy Glick's hero story stuck with me. He was on the plane that hit the ground in Pennsylvania. He called his wife after hearing other passengers talking about other planes that were crashed. She verified that was true and he explained that he and two others were going to do something to the hijackers. He told her to stay on the phone and he gave the phone to his Dad. She heard screams, and then silence. Jeremy's mom said he always wanted to be a superhero. He got his wish! I was so grateful to him, truly a hero. I wondered what I would have done on that plane. Probably nothing, maybe that is why he was on that plane. The additional lives that he saved because that plane didn't reach its intended destination brought him to a status beyond superhero in my mind. I knew one lady who was in Building One and when she knew there was an issue, she grabbed her purse and got out of there. There are stories of so many people who were supposed to be in there, who just didn't make it to work that day. I believe all the people lost in this 9/11 tragedy had a dialogue with God before they arrived here on Earth; they knew they would pass that day. EVERY single one of them made this day one that will live in history as the day we stood up against hatred. This day was one that has changed many things for the better, and without this event, it would not have happened as quickly. We need to remember that every person has their own individual life path. We don't know how we are all interconnected, but we all have a reason for being here. Doing distance Reiki helps those who need it, and gives us a better understanding of why things happen. I had reservations about whether I should try to even send Bin Laden Reiki, however, he is human, and I hoped I could help in some small way. This was the beginning of my desire to send Reiki to any one whom I thought could use it around the world.

Bin Laden underestimated the power of love. It brought America together. Love united people to overcome evil. Bin Laden didn't understand the depth of the power of love, as he never experienced it. For those of faith, it made them stronger to go without their loved ones in physicality, but with a deeper spiritual understanding and determination to make changes for a better world. All 5,422 people who passed are heroes, making the power of love so much greater than any hate could ever be in this world. They stood up for LOVE! My heart is filled with gratitude and I am so humbled. Reiki has given me the ability to look at situations from a totally different perspective, I am in awe of ALL THAT IS.

Reflection: We, as light workers, will always be needed to send love and light to those who are not promoting a world where everyone is accepted everywhere. Since then, I have sent love to the world daily. I choose rose quartz, Herkimer diamond, clear quartz, tiger iron, and black tourmaline. I start my meditation by asking God to bring me the love I need to heal me. I ask him to send Jesus and any entity of the light and unconditional love to sit in the back of my heart and heal every atom, cell, fiber, muscle and organ. Once I feel it has been done, I then send it to my whole family, extended family, friends, neighbors and state. Then move it across America, and to the whole world. Sometimes I see myself handing out heart shaped red balloons to everyone. At other times when I feel I don't have a lot of time I will put rose quartz on an image of the world and Reiki it and ask that it continue to heal Mother Earth for 24 hours at a time. Remember the high vibration of LOVE is able to overcome the negative vibration of hate. Keep sending love, especially to those who are of a lower vibration! More and more Reiki and prayers are needed as the world is coming closer and closer to being one loving world! Please remember to protect yourself first!

September 17, 2001

I become a REIKI MASTER!!! Although I am now official, I felt I had this ability before the official class. My Reiki Master explains to me that this is called Advanced Reiki class, and it is what she received as a Master as well. Various Reiki lineages called it different names, and I am perfectly happy with whatever the title is! There is a huge sense of responsibility that comes with this title and I feel honored to become a Master! Little did I know of the additional years of work that it would take for me to actually BE a Reiki Master and know it from a soul perspective, and living it every day! My experience has helped me grow as a person, to understand healing in a way I never thought possible. It has opened my mind to natural healing as

I witness the powerful AH-HA moments again and again. It is an awesome moment when you are connected with something greater than you, and you feel it spiritually in your soul. I know this is why I am here, to spread this to as many people as I can in my life time. This is my passion!

My Reiki 1 Practitioner book has this quote in it from Albert Einstein: "Great Spirits have always encountered violent opposition from mediocre minds." My mother was my first violent opposition to Reiki. She lived with us and when people would come over for Reiki class, she would go out for the day. I knew that by using Reiki in the house, it would slowly get to her, but it took years. She was raised Catholic and attended Catholic schools with nuns. When I first explained what it was, she said "Who do you think you are, God?" and dismissed me. It was hurtful; I thought how can you raise a daughter, love everything she does, say you are proud of her and then not even listen to the possibilities? She had a closed mind and didn't take into consideration that I could possibly have a way to help heal her. I was baffled that she believed she raised me as a "good girl" and yet somewhere I went "bad." I cried many nights, talking to God and asking him to help me show her the light.

Many years passed before she allowed me to Reiki her arthritis in her hands so she could crochet. She commented that it felt like I was using Ben Gay, and ta-da, she FINALLY realized the benefit! Thereafter, she would ask me to use my Ben Gay hands on her. I was happy she allowed the huge shift in thinking, of at least this one topic.

Reflection: Many Reiki Practitioners experience violent opposition from family members. I believe they are afraid something is changing and Reiki will make you pull away from them. When you simply explain that it is a natural healing technique that everyone can benefit from, that helps. In my Mom's eyes, it was a huge issue because it was not "discovered" by Jesus Christ. I had to talk about the fact that Jesus healed with his hands; how are we to know if this is not what he used? The main point Mom was trying to make was that Jesus could do miracles and was a deity. There was no way in her mind that I would be able to be like him. I told her, "I never said I was like him, you did." I explained "this helped me be closer to God and Jesus, and although I can't heal exactly like him, wouldn't it be good if this helped you a little bit?" I then told her it can't hurt you, it comes from God, and God is love. I think this conversation helped to move her into the right direction of trying it. Once they try it, they can (and generally do) agree it is a good thing!

Angel's know real love conquers all. This is something that resonates so deeply with me; it comes up over and over in my life. In October, 2001 a client was becoming emotionally detached from her husband and she talked about leaving him. I convinced her that she should only leave if she was sure there was no way to reconcile. I gave her the angel message "real love conquers all," and I explained she needed to seriously consider what her true intentions and thoughts were for their relationship. Life proceeds out of intention. At this point, she didn't know. I said "at this point your intentions are already driving this relationship into the ground, instead of uplifting it." She said, "it is a two way street." I told her she hasn't tried hard enough, neither has he. She needed to rely on God. I believe that we choose to come back to Earth with our husbands, partners and family to lift each other higher. If we are angels, or aspire to be like them, we will not give up and only LOVE will conquer this issue. Not mind games, money or children- love of and for each other. I felt that whey they finally reconnected the love they felt it in their hearts when they first married that they would physically realize it and act and show it differently. I have seen this work with others and I hoped it would work with her as well. Intention is what drives everything from our emotions to our actions. It is hard work, but I pushed her to dig deeper into her emotions today. I encouraged her to seek professional help as they need to communicate.

Reflection: Too many times anger leads to resentment and betrayal. Couples need to be able to air their emotions to each other in order to heal. I have a magnet on my fridge that says "don't go to sleep with an argument unsettled." There have been long nights at my house, but to keep a relationship working, you both have to work at it. At first, people are angry and yell at each other, blaming the other person as they understand the story from their own perspective. Then, silence takes over as each one tries to come to grips with their emotions and also see the other side of the argument. Sometimes one partner breaks out of the silence before the other one and starts the emotional confrontation. Whoever it is, they need to be able to vocalize feelings coming from the heart. This is how arguments end, the heart knows the answers, go there.

How do you rely on God? Prayers do it. Faith that he is listening to the prayers is important. Noticing signs along the way is helpful to reinforce your faith. It works in a circle, you pray, you listen, you notice. Then you start again with more prayer and say thanks for the sign you noticed. You are now relying on God for more signs and as your intuition opens up more, the signs become easier to recognize and become more frequent. I have prayed for the smallest thing like needing a new nightstand at a reasonable price. Once you put it out there, know the prayer was heard, and know it will be done. I happened to be looking for another item in a small antique store and mentioned how pretty this small round table was, the owner says, "it's yours for $20" WOW! That was a bargain I couldn't refuse! It was not even why I was there. These are the times when you know God was listening and put you in the right place at the right time!

A friend sees lady bugs as a reminder of her sister who passed. She doesn't believe in messages, but slowly she is noticing the lady bugs keep showing up! One day she had a disagreement with a friend and went shopping. She finds a shirt covered in lady bugs, giving her support and encouragement that the disagreement wasn't that bad, that she needs to focus on the big picture! Now she listens to messages!

I am not sure if it was because of my lack of confidence or concern about having enough energy, but I decided to teach classes in 2 four hour classes with a week in-between them. I teach small classes of 3 or less in order to keep within this four hour time frame. However this started out, I believe another reason I need to teach this way is to allow the student time to practice. I remember when I got my Reiki 1 attunements and was sent home, never to contact my Reiki Master again. In my mind, that had to change as I had sooooo many additional questions after the class and wanted to be able to have more conversations. I feel that the first class with 2 attunements gives the client time to adjust to the energy and time to practice on family and friends to come back with additional questions the following week. The first four hour class is intense for those who have never had any energy work, and is enough to excite them without over stressing their system. Reiki 2 class is held the same way, and my Reiki Master Teacher class is about a year due to all the things you need to learn besides having the attunements.

Many people call upon different deities to bring in energy before giving Reiki. God is always first on my list. I know he will be sure to keep my healing energy clear, unconditionally loving and constant. Next, I ask Jesus, Mary, Joseph, and Anna to come help me. I ask Seraph Rose Aura, Archangels Michael, Raphael, Gabriel and Uriel to help and of course Dr. Usui and Mrs. Takata are normally there before I even begin class. I also invite any unconditionally loving ancestors to join me. Whoever you invite, please be sure they love you unconditionally and are of the light. If you are not sure, ask three times to get a positive response or tell them they are not wanted and must leave or go to the light. There are good and bad energies out there! Please be sure you are only working with the ones who want to help manifest more healing in this world.

Because of the fear of turning people away from Reiki, back when I first started giving Reiki, we were instructed to use the words "universal life energy" to describe it. It certainly is, but I know it's coming to me from God, and I finally got comfortable saying it. I believe you are getting exactly what you need every time you receive Reiki. I don't know what that is, nor do I need to know what it is, I believe God will work with you on your own timeline to heal it. If you want healing with the very first treatment, you will get it. If there is hesitance in your belief, there will be hesitance in your healing. FAITH in your God is what heals you. You have to release all fear, surrender to his unconditional love for you and be willing to receive what is yours. The thoughts that you have make it happen, so stay positive any time you are getting work done!

In October, a faithful, religious person told me she believed in one God, and you pray to him through Jesus' name. "There are no other Gods, "she said. She didn't believe in angels, Quan Yin, Buddha, or anyone else. She said you don't need them, you just pray to Jesus. She put down Reiki by saying those who come to us don't have faith in God so it's better to at least believe in this than nothing. I needed to understand her viewpoint. But it got worse, I asked her if I prayed to anyone but Jesus if the prayers would work, she said "no, that's why there won't be world peace, because everyone isn't praying to Jesus." She believed she is a sinner and needs Jesus to forgive her. This whole conversation put me and Reiki in a bad light, and ruined our relationship, as I could not believe only in her way, so she would no longer converse with me. This was the first time I was mind boggled. She never asked me if I believed in God or Jesus, she assumed I had no faith, as I don't belong to a church. Her mind was so closed off to the possibility that I could have faith and through me, God is healing people. She could not understand that I could believe in Jesus or not and still be friends with me. I was glad that she taught me a huge lesson; I just wish she had understood it from my point of view. I believe in God, and know that God is the purest form of unconditional love; I forgave her and wished her the best.

Reflection: Everyone has different religious beliefs. It hurts me that world peace is not a basic belief that everyone can agree upon. I pray to God, Jesus, Buddha, and any deity of unconditional love who can help, for world peace daily - even multiple times a day. Prayers of good intention, in my opinion, count! Don't stop sending prayers of hope, peace and love. Universal energy of peace is available to all!

Reiki is not a religion, but can actually enhance your connection to Spirit. It doesn't matter WHO you believe in. I have friends of several different religions all practicing Reiki with their belief system; they are all using Reiki to find new depths to what they believe. Like adding whipped cream to my favorite hot cocoa, it just makes it sweeter!

Do you have to believe in God to do Reiki? NO, but let me tell you how incredibly close to God you do feel. You are part of him. It only enhances whatever you do believe. And, it works even if you don't believe...isn't that the most amazing thing ever? I once gave Reiki to a man who was atheist. He had asked me if I believed in God and I told him it didn't matter what I believed, Reiki works with what YOU believe. I am just the "channel" thru which you will get what you need to heal. That was acceptable to him and since he believed in science, it was easy for him to understand Universal Energy. His mind was open enough to allow the experience. That's all you need for Reiki to work, the person just has to say "yes, I'll try it."

October 21, 2001

Two clients attend Reiki 1 class. During an attunement, one said she felt me touch her head and it felt like at that moment she saw a great white light. She said she got really hot as if the sun where blasting her! I wanted to be able to do that; had asked for her to see the light, and she did!!!! Now the interesting part is that when giving attunements, the guides are really giving the person what they need, but the RM's intentions must play a big part of it as well. EVERY time I ask for something specific to happen, it does....I am awestruck!!

Later, when the client was on the table she said she had 40 stitches in the right knee. As I gave her Reiki it began to twitch. I took out my stones: citrine, and held it under her knee and used lepidolite and sodalite on the top of the knee. These are not typical stones to use for this chakra, but intuition was guiding me this way, so why not? Her knee starts jumping and she said she felt as if someone was sticking a needle into it. She asked what we were doing as the pain was intense. I explained it may get worse before it gets better. But to please let us finish if she could stand the pain. We assured her it needed to leave, and she agreed. Next, she felt hot as we both placed our hands on top of each other. I asked her if she believed we could heal it, "yes" she replied. Then I told her to ask for her Mom and Dad, God and angels, spirit guides, Archangel Raphael (for healing) and people who were of the light and unconditional love that had passed before her to help with the healing. As each one came, she cried. We explained the spirits all can help her at any time; all she needs to do is ask. It took time for the pain to subside, but when she finally had a change of mind and allowed the healing; her knee felt the best it ever did once she stood up on it! It's important to note that she wanted it to heal. If for ANY reason the client doesn't know, or believes that it can't be healed this way, then it won't be healed. The mind and heart have to be in agreement. This could be why some people don't heal as quickly as others.

Reflection: Many times I have heard Practitioners say they stop giving Reiki when it becomes painful for the client. This is the time when you need to push through it, as you are removing the original issue. I always ask the client to try and help me get rid of the issue. Give the client a selenite stick and ask them to take the pain out of the area with it. If you get the client involved with their own healing, it happens faster! It's important to ask the client if they want it healed. Their faith in the healing makes it happen faster. And very infrequently, the client will say they are learning something from it, and may not be ready to heal yet. Either way, it's important to understand, they have free will. And their will, will be done.

May 2, 2002

I woke up with a tight feeling around my arm, like someone died of a heart attack. I get sensations in my body and have to ask what it means. Typically, a tight arm is a symptom of a heart attack, yet I could not tell who it was that was having it. I knew it was not me as I had no other symptoms. I had an appointment at 6:30pm and while there, my friend's husband came in and said his father just died of a heart attack. I didn't know the father, and barely knew the husband. I didn't connect the two events immediately, and when I finally did, I didn't know what to think of it. Why was I being given this info if I couldn't do anything about it? If I didn't even know WHO it was, how could I use it? I thought about the fact that I wanted to change this appointment all week, and couldn't due to conflicting schedules. I was supposed to be there when it happened. I was able to offer some words of comfort, and was a buffer in that moment. This person was of a different religion than I and after talking with another friend, she told me I can't even send prayers to her and her family, as they wouldn't receive them. Now, I am beginning to wonder if there is yet another issue I should be addressing. If I can't even send sincere wishes to a friend of another religion, how can world peace exist? I decide I need to talk to my RM, who told me that I was being condescending, trying to get people to see things from a different perspective. I thought that's what we were already doing, especially with distance Reiki. I now am wondering where I stand in this field, and if there is even a place for me. My emotions are all over the place and I am totally lost. People have to want change in order for it to happen; in the meantime, I just wanted to be able to talk to people with open minds. And it seems that is not happening yet. I am starting to understand that some people are in your life for reasons like teaching you lessons. I never thought about the fact that people with various religious backgrounds can't all be friends in the way that I am accustomed. There has to be a way that we can all connect, aren't all religions based on love? Isn't unconditional love a universal need for humans to not only exist, but thrive? I am beginning to think too many people have conditions on what love is, and where or whom it should come from. If love is unconditional, it doesn't judge.

Reflection: If you have any symptoms of a heart attack, please call 911 for emergency assistance. While energy work can mimic life threatening events, it's best to have professionals rule out any medical issues.

July 23, 2002

A returning client is making amazing progress with her own issues. She recognizes that her anger is an issue. I told her of the saying from author Debbie Ford: "the reflection in the mirror sends the light back to you to find the answer." We talked in great length about her past. I asked her when she was going to break this cycle. I explained about my Miraculous Mary Medal in silver helps with patience. She was able to use silver for patience and completing tasks. She was amazed!

Reflection: In my Reiki 2 class we use a list of words from The Dark Side of the Light Chasers by Debbie Ford to eliminate the emotion behind the words that get a reaction from you. Once you remove the emotion, the anger is gone and you can address the real issue from a calm place. Once you can focus just on facts, the answers come quickly. You need to be able to remove emotion to heal and forgive any situation that is giving you pain. Sometimes this takes a lot of time, and effort. Writing a list of why you are angry helps. I generally make my list and then burn it asking God to bring the conflict within me to a calm energy. I do a lot of reflecting and try to see the issue from the other side as well. As my favorite singer Phil Collins song reminds me, "We always need to hear both sides of the story." You may be amazed at the insight you receive in a time of need when you listen for intuition to kick in. Give thanks and burn the letter knowing God or Universal Energy will handle the situation for you. Feel the calm within.

October 2002

One Sunday I felt like a truck hit me. I felt weak, my legs felt like a wet noodles. I stayed in my PJ's and didn't go anywhere. I felt like someone died, I was so drained. On Wednesday, I got a phone call that an Aunt had passed on Tuesday night! She had everyone over for dinner on the previous Sunday, told everyone where the wrapped Christmas gifts were, which clothes to keep, who to give stuff to, etc. She knew she wasn't going to be around much longer. Now I know that my feelings are definitely a sign that someone is passing, and I need to ask very specific questions about who it is and if there is anything I can do. I sent her distant Reiki and talked with her about Heaven. She said no one here is in a hurry, there's nothing to be nervous about, as she was talking in a very calm voice. I asked my Aunt to please reach out to my Mom to let her know that she's ok. This is the first time I talked with someone who recently passed, and it will become common soon. I hope that my feeling weak will become less intense so I don't have to miss work, but I guess this was the only way for me to recognize and connect the feeling to her passing.

Reflection: I am noticing each time this happens, another step is revealed. If it happened all at once, I would have thought I needed to see a doctor. The doctor surely would prescribe medicine and I wouldn't progress as my soul intended. God and the angels work with you to ensure you get only what you need at the time. They understand we are in physical bodies and need to be able to physically catch up to what is emotionally or spiritually taking place.

I worked for a small company where I was told I needed to get a back bone. There came a point where I needed more compensation for the work I was doing and I told the boss about it in March. He ignored my request until the last moment when I said I found another job. I told him I finally found my back bone. I then thought about this event which happened earlier in March. I was going to a seminar with a co-worker and slipped and fell on ice in the parking lot. I stayed on the ground for a good 5 minutes before getting up. My co-worker got worried and said she was calling an ambulance, I said no. I just need to get back into my body. My soul was not connected to my physical body and this was the very first time this happened. I was floating above my body and could not feel my physical body. I finally started praying, "Dear God, please bring me back into my physical body, heal me to be 100% healthy. Thank you, Amen." When I finally got up, I was absolutely fine. I had to wonder if this was readjusting my back bone. Looking back, of course it was healing the physical body so the mental body could also adjust. People who have accidents should consider what else is off in their life. Accidents happen for a reason!

Reflection: Have you noticed that the previous diary entries from March, May, and July are all about words? I notice that when I need to learn a lesson, it happens three times to get my attention. Pay attention to words people say to you. This boss meant I had no backbone when it came to work issues. He thought I wouldn't stand up for myself. At that time, he was right, but when I finally got it, he didn't like my reaction to it. Also, pay attention to words you say to others. People tend to speak quickly without thinking about the words coming out of their mouths. This is what is most detrimental to society as a whole. When someone questions you, it's ok to think about the answer before responding. I would rather tell the person "I need a moment to think about that" then just say random negativity back. Once you put words out there that are not from the heart, it can be difficult to ever get back to the point before you spoke those words. My tip is to do a self-diagnostic observation. You know you should not speak if your heart is racing, this means you have enormous amount of negative energy around the subject. In this case, you are bound to say something you don't mean. It's okay to excuse yourself and find a quiet place to contemplate your response. When you finally have the correct response, and your heart is calm, then you can continue the conversation. In this world where everyone is connected to each other instantly with cell phones and messaging, it's best to know in your heart when to respond and when to walk away.

June 16, 2003

I have been giving Reiki to a client who was dealing with a cancerous lymph node under her right arm. She had no feeling in her right hand. Today I got her to feel tingling in her fingers! I am hoping things are starting to move. I gave her my selenite stick and kyanite, I knew she needed them, and I didn't even think about it, I just did it. I hope if she ever decided to get rid of them that I would get them back, they mean so much to me.

Reflection: Rocks come and go with me. Some are meant to be with others and I either give them away or I lose them. I pick up stones on vacation and bring them back to the house to add to my flower garden. The energy there is like a relaxing vacation! Each rock has a different vibration to it. In order to feel, sense, or know it, put the rock in the palm of your hand and lovingly talk to it. Ask it if it wants to help you heal, or simply come to your house to be a decorative stone. Take a moment to listen, it will tell you!

January 2006

I read <u>Peace, Love and Healing</u> by Bernie Siegel, MD. I finally got the message I should have known a long time ago. I don't have to fix everyone's problems. I just need to be there while THEY figure it out. Maybe God gives me people with issues to help them find God. By Labor Day, I still feel bad that I can't fix other people's problems. However, I know that with Reiki, everyone has a closer connection with their God, and that alone is enough to propel me forward.

Reflection: I would replay this lesson over and over again until I really peeled back several more layers over many more years to really understand it. I can explain why I think things happen to people in their life. However, they have to be willing to do the work necessary to make a permanent change. This one thing is NOT something anyone has control over but themselves. Each individual is on their path, and has free will to BE anything they want to be. I am trying to BE love. Maybe that is enough to help.

February 2008

My sons both get Reiki 1 Practitioner attunements. They are young enough to absorb it naturally without any preconceived ideas. Later in the year, we were in a card store and they sold candles with money inside them. One son stood at this display and used Reiki on every candle to find the one with the highest denomination in it. Sure enough, when he burned it, there was a fifty dollar bill inside! Now I never would have thought to even do that, but children think outside the box! Later in life, we use Reiki on college applications to ensure getting into the college of choice. And of course, it works!

7/14/2010

Southington Reiki, LLC is born! The grand opening was 8/1/10 in our home basement! It was previously used for the kid's desks, and now that they've outgrown the space, it was time for it to become a Reiki room. I figured out the Feng Shui map and started placing stuff in the room. I am amazed at how natural this is for me to put together. So many things in my home belong in this space, and it all flows beautifully! My son made Reiki stencils to paint them on the walls, and it feels sacred now. The Grand Opening told me I was on the right track. A few friends attended, and everyone received a free Reiki treatment! A person attended who was the doubting Thomas about Reiki up until now. In previous conversations she told me "If I don't believe it will work, then it won't." I tried hard to understand why she wouldn't believe it doesn't work. She said "there is no proof" and this was years before current proof has come along. I said "there's no proof of miracles either, yet they happen." I asked her, "Do you believe in miracles?" With no response, I assumed not. A lot of what you believe or allow into your mind is what occurs. If you let your mind be open to the possibilities of miracles, you will see and get them. I had told her that there is a line that everyone crosses and becomes a believer; I hoped to get her across the line, and we did! How did this work? I believe after YEARS of me talking about Reiki, she finally was ok with me working on her. Although still very hesitant, her mind was open to it. Your Soul knows what it needs to heal, even if you don't. Your soul is just waiting for you to allow the natural, loving, and healing energy to begin. She is not emotional in front of people, yet I saw the glimmer in her eye. It said: "Wow, you didn't tell me it would be this wonderful." I felt like I finally proved myself to her as something just shifted in our relationship. She said that she normally had to take a muscle relaxer in the am and pm in order to survive the day. This had been her ritual for years. She had not taken any medicine for 5 days, and she was simply beyond words. It reminded me of the quote by Unknown: "There will be haters, there will be doubters, there will be non-believers, and then there will be YOU proving them wrong." I have felt this way ever since starting Reiki. I feel like there are so many people out there with no faith in God and his ability to heal through others. This was the blessing I had hoped for, something to encourage me to keeping moving in this direction. One by one, we can help heal them, and teach them to heal others too!

Reflection: As of the year 2016, she still doesn't have the back pain she used to have previously. When going for a Reiki session, be open to the possibility of receiving your own healing miracles. Be mindful of where the Practitioner's hands are, and use your prayers and intentions to get what you need. Your Practitioner can tell you what they are working on as they go and you can pray at that time for your highest and greatest healing at each chakra.

March 15, 2011

My widowed client had a car accident leaving her with neck, shoulder, and back issues. When giving her crown chakra Reiki, it had some warmth, and she talked about being mad at God. She hasn't been to church in over a year and I suggest she go when there is no mass to just sit and talk with God, as this is the communication chakra that's bothering her. She admits she is holding onto the grief and feels guilty about it. She is stuck here and doesn't want to go back to the church. She needs to find a way to release this so that her health gets back on track. I see this one thing as the major issue holding her back from balance. I explained that her husband's path in life was complete, but she was still here to continue on. She needed to make peace with her God and recognize how precious her life still is even though she is without him. I felt bad, as although it was crystal clear to me what she needed to do, she wasn't ready to return to God. All I can do is continue to send her Reiki and loving prayers and be here should she return.

Reflection: It is extremely difficult to know what people need and not be able to convince them to try something. I know she needs an emotional release in order to find the balance within, but that is not something she can understand right now. We all experience loss in our lives. It hurts our heart horribly. We feel we can't go on. We question why we are left after they are gone. The answer is because each soul has a goal to accomplish. Once that goal is achieved, they can leave. It is overwhelming to think that you now have to continue on alone. Pray to God, ask to find the answers you are looking for then listen and notice the signs. I often tell people if they are coming to me, there is a reason. Listen to your intuition, listen to your soul. They are giving you a message, trust and follow it.

April 1, 2011

Every day since becoming a Reiki Master, I learn something new. I have had receding gums and have been using Reiki on them along with my stomach. I just read in a Reiki book, <u>Hand to Hand</u> from Harvey Gray, to Reiki the teeth and shoulders together....wow, what a difference. I had no idea my shoulders needed it, until I tried it! Two months ago I also eliminated gluten from my diet. Sometimes I get a small headache, but I treat it with Reiki and it goes away quickly. My gums look healthy again and the dentist asked what I am doing differently....I tell her I Reiki them and just get a look of "ok, I don't believe that is it." When will this doubting end?

Reflection: I have always known I could heal myself; I just really had to focus on the issue at hand. This doesn't mean just once, this means a dedicated effort for a few months before seeing the dentist.

I joined a networking group this month and hope that it's the direction I need to go in to get my Reiki business off the ground. One of the members took the Reiki 1 class, and I can tell she was hesitant about whether it could really help her or not. After her first two attunements she wasn't sure if she had Reiki or not. I asked what could be causing the heat in her hands if it wasn't Reiki, and she didn't know. It's interesting to me, that most people believe that if you can't see it, you don't trust it. The following week she said that she had time to practice during the week and got rid of the carpal tunnel pain in her hands! After her second two attunements she said she felt awesome and couldn't wait to practice on her family and friends.

April 2, 2011

I met this lady who was talking about going to see someone for Reiki in another town. She was in the healing industry and wanted to add this practice to her offerings. We talked and I had her over for a free Reiki session. Her half hour session lead me to ground her to Mother Earth. I used a meditation to direct the energy up her legs, all the way to crown chakra. She admits that her energy is scattered all over the place, and I am able to successfully bring her back to balance.

July 2011

A client came to me and she tells me she thinks I was the Goddess Isis in a past life. Isis is known for helping cure people and feathered friends. Her followers gave her roses —I love roses! This doesn't feel logical to me; Why would I be here in CT and not some big city doing greater work if this were true? Birds hibernate at night to conserve energy, and I feel bone chilling cold as I fall asleep. I wonder if that is to show me my connection with birds. Years ago a friend asked me if I was to be a bird, which one I would be. It took a bit to recognize that I had seagulls in various places…… once I looked up seagull, I knew it was correct! Animal guides are amazing at showing us our strengths and weaknesses! I use Ted Andrews' book Animal Speak when an animal shows up in my life.

July 8, 2011

A client purchased Reiki sessions for her Dad for arthritis in his knees and he has a hard time walking. At the time, my Reiki studio was down a flight of stairs. It became obvious that he had issues while watching him put one foot on a step and then bring the other foot down to the same step. It took time for him to get down the ten steps and was clearly painful. Before the session began, I asked what his goal was for the Reiki session. He replied "to sit on the floor and play with my grandchildren." I explained that may take more than one session, but let's see how we do today and work from there! When starting the Reiki session, I intuitively started at his feet, since he is having issues walking it felt like I needed to start here. I find, in general, men also prefer starting Reiki at the feet, as it feels less threatening to them than starting anywhere else. I stood in this one position for 15 minutes with extreme sweating of my hands on his feet. I went up to both knees at the same time, then to his hips, stomach, hands, elbows, shoulders, head and then asked him to flip over as my back was hurting. I used an iridized rock on his back and my hands were tingly at his hard heart chakra. I went back down his body to the feet for another 15 minutes. When done I asked him to sit up slowly and gave him a bottle of water to drink. He said, "It was amazing!" He couldn't believe the range of motion he now had moving his legs just off the Reiki table. He said he felt better than he has in years! "This is why I do this" I told him. It makes my heart happy to know I can really help make someone feel well in just an hour!

He returned four days later for the second session. I rarely use stones or crystals during the first Reiki session as I want the client to get used to just the Reiki energy. If they have had Reiki before, I will ask if I can use stones, as I prefer Reiki with the extra healing energy! I asked him what pain level he was at before the first session- absolute 10, and after 1. For two days following the first session he had less pain and then it started to return again. I instructed him to return as soon as the pain did because we would be able to get rid of it faster. During this second session I explain we will use stones to enhance the Reiki. He's holding a selenite stick in the right hand to remove negative energy and a blue kyanite stick in the left hand to open all chakras. I am using a Green Chlorite Phantom stone to specifically work on self-healing and regeneration. This time my hands were not as hot on his feet and I worked more on the left side than anywhere else. This is the side where he is allowing more energy in, connecting with his feminine side of healing. I heard and felt big bubbles rising to the surface. This is how I know the energy blockages are moving, and take this as a great sign of healing. As this was happening, he complained of knee pain, and I asked that he allow me to continue to move the energy, unless it was so unbearable that I had to stop. I explained this needs to be removed for him to feel better. He agreed and said he felt much better when I was done. His daughter said that he is moving more like a 20 year old instead of the 85 year old that he felt like with the pain.

After the 3rd session, he had no pain in his knees at all. In September, he returned for more Reiki and the sessions continued to get deeper into his tissues. I felt the energy of my hands reaching further down into the tissues, where before the energy was closer to the top. I had been working on his back, but couldn't find where the initial pain was coming from, he told me the hip. Once I had the correct location, I kept one hand there and one hand at his foot. He was very uncomfortable for a few minutes as his legs would spasm and stiffen up. He complained when he came in that he worked during the day putting in doors and his back hurt. By the time we were done, the pain in the back was gone! The week before we had worked on the right leg, this time I had the same reaction except it wasn't up to his hip, just to the thigh. He returned after eight sessions in October and I felt before he arrived this one would be about strengthening. The past two were removing energy blockages in the legs, and tonight I used the Merlin stone at his head and my hands were hot for 15 minutes. He fell asleep and woke as I was on the right leg. I explained we were strengthening and doing maintenance now. He is able to walk up and down stairs normally! He said he went to work today, and was able to lift boxes. He then went to the store with his granddaughter and walked around the store twice, and went up and down stairs! He was now able to sit on the floor with his granddaughter, and I had tears of joy in my eyes! To be able to give this to someone brought me an incredible sense of purpose to my heart! He and his daughter took the Reiki 1 Practitioner class together! Nothing made me happier than to know he met his goal!!! I helped him transform his dream into wellness!

Reflection: Once I get the condition healed, I highly recommend the client learn Reiki as they can now handle the vibrational upkeep. Many times people come to me as a last resort. They have been to doctors and have had all the recommended medicines, with no benefit. My sincere hope is that people start using Reiki at a younger age, know when to use Reiki on their pain and can maintain their health with their doctor's guidance. I often wonder about moms who teach their children to use Reiki at any early age. Will those children be at the doctor with medical issues as frequently as those without Reiki?

July 14, 2011

A client asked if I'd do a session outside during the full moon. WOW! This was a first. Why didn't I think of this before? We started at 7:15pm, and she picked out a record keeper to use as we are doing the session. Many believe that the record keeper triangles can used to access information that's been stored within the crystal. These crystals have also been shown to activate dormant intuitive abilities and enhance ones psychic skills. She places it on her third eye chakra, so I begin Reiki here. Within five minutes, the Reiki is incredibly hot, not sweaty. Then it was as if the record keeper opened the third eye chakra by bursting into a flame. I saw this with my eyes open, and actually jumped back since this has never happened before! It was so hot! I just sat there and waited for it to cool down. I believe it helped to clear a blockage that was keeping her intuition at bay. The rest of the session was very average; I'd almost say that it was not needed. The important part was done at the beginning at the third eye. She said she thought the stone was going to leave a mark on her forehead!

Reflection: Reiki sessions during full moons are most powerful. Try it!

July 23, 2011

A husband and wife take Reiki 1 Practitioner class together. The wife had shared that she didn't believe in anything. During both attunements on her, my heart raced and it took several minutes for it to return to a normal heart beat. Reiki has a way of softening a heart. During the week they practiced on each other and I asked her to hold rose quartz during the last two attunements. These go much easier and I was happy that I didn't feel the extreme heart beats this time. We used a healing sounds cd as we worked on each of them, and my sinuses were tingling while working on both of them, and they said they didn't notice a difference. I know they continued to use this healing method on every day aches and pains, and that may be all they needed! I notice that before giving attunements, I can't eat much of anything. Strawberries and grapes was all I wanted, but about an hour after, I am starving for food! I find I am drinking so much more water now to keep hydrated!

Reflection: More couples should take Reiki together! The few couples who do are able to heal each other. What an amazing gift to be able to share!

August 17, 2011

This client says she doesn't feel like herself lately. She grew up with crystals and meditation but lost it along the way. Tonight brought her back to meditation and she had a great experience when I asked her to put all her negative energy into a briefcase. She pictured pouring negative stuff into in and shredding it. She also has a shoulder issue, which I explained is related to communication, and she admitted there is stuff she wants to say without being mean about it. She saw black birds coming out of her mouth. I recommended she read up on black birds in the Ted Andrews book: <u>Animal Speak</u>. Black birds mean a new understanding of nature as they come into your life. It is always amazing how the information in his book can help your situation. I always remember to look up animals that I see during the day for words of guidance.

September 18, 2011

This client has seen her doctor and he told her she needs knee replacement surgery. She thought she'd try Reiki and at first the Reiki energy moved so slowly, it took half an hour to move the energy from her foot to knee. There are definite circulation issues here and we do visualization for her to connect to Mother Earth quicker. I ask her to imagine standing at a beach, with her feet at the edge of the water. Her feet sink into the sand and the water splashes up over her feet. As her feet sink further into the sand, I ask her to start talking to Mother Earth, asking for the energy she needs to heal to come up into the bottoms of her feet. I ask her to envision this as a ball of red energy that is limitless and she can get as much as she needs, knowing that Mother Earth will only give her what she needs. This seems to help the energy flow in easier and quicker. I tell her that she needs to carry stones for arthritis, turquoise and copper, as well as first chakra stones, red jasper, and some black tourmaline stones for grounding. Also, I got the message she needs to wear better shoes for the job she does…. "oh yeah," she says, "I've been meaning to look into that!" I am personally starting to notice a trend….once I have two people with the same issue, there is likely to be a third to really make an impact on my knowledge of the issue.

Reflection: I asked her how much red she wore, and not surprisingly, "never" was the answer. I am always recommending colors that people should wear. IF there is a specific chakra they are trying to heal, it is so important to incorporate that color in everything they do. Wear it in clothing and jewelry, sleep in that color sheets, eat and drink it as much as possible. You can even purchase plastic color therapy glasses and wear them 10 to 30 minutes a day. You are reinforcing the subconscious mind that you are supporting the healing process.

October 23, 2011

Three clients take Reiki 1 Practitioner Class! This class was thrown together at the last minute. I had originally announced a class for Saturday and no one signed up. So I changed it to Sunday and three people attended! They all felt comfortable together and shared the same leg circulation issue. During the first attunement my heart was racing and I knew heart chakras were opening. It was 74 degrees in the Reiki studio and those of us working on one of the clients were cold. Cold is felt when you are removing inflammation, but you stay in the position, and then the hands turn to warm to heal the cells. This is similar to the icy hot packs.

Reflection: I typically have Reiki 1 and 2 Practitioner books ready for class so that I can have an impromptu class at any time. This one thing makes my day go smoothly if I don't have to slow down to do this task right before the class!

November 16, 2011

This client was the easiest person I have ever attuned! I was actually worried I didn't do it properly, it went so smoothly! At the end of the attunement, I sit and allow the person to meditate as long as they need to, since this is the most important part of the class. Most of the time people are so excited to tell you what they saw, however she didn't say anything after the first two attunements, which also made me doubt I did it correctly. After all the attunements were done she shared that she saw Jesus all four times. During the fourth attunement, she saw a white light. She has anxiety attacks so bad that she sometimes doesn't leave her house. She was sure a part of the past was with her. She had released it in the past but felt the need to release again before the last attunement. I gave her privacy for 10 minutes and she felt better upon my return. When I did the 4th attunement, I asked that she be shown the light and that she heal the past to move on as a confident well protected woman. I was given the message that she was protected by God. We talked about protecting yourself by calling in Archangel Michael. The prayer is simple and can be used for protecting yourself, house, car, flight, etc…

Lord Michael above me
Lord Michael below me
Lord Michael to the left of me
Lord Michael to the right of me

Lord Michael, Lord Michael, where ever I go.

I am his love protecting here.

I am his love protecting here.

I am his love protecting here.

Please watch over me (insert other names here) and get us home safely no matter what means of transportation we take at the end of the day.

Thank you Lord Michael, Amen.

November 2011

I get a forwarded email from a member of a networking group. She mentions the lady in the email is selling her business and is selling all her store merchandise, "maybe there is something you could use," she said. I read the entire email and blurted out, "I am going to buy this business!" Then I spun my head around to see who said that, because it wasn't me! I reread the email a few more times and decided I needed to at least see it, to find out why she is selling it, etc. I prayed to God for guidance, as I didn't know how to run a business on my own. What I did know is that I loved Reiki and it needed a home. I was already working a full time job but knew that my passion wasn't in it. I was hopeful that this new venture would allow me to quit the other job. I opened A Hand in Healing on January 4, 2012! Feeling excited yet nervous about what was ahead, I prayed daily for the energy to be able to do both jobs, and I got it!

March 2012

A client came for Reiki 2 Practitioner class. Although this is not taught in traditional Reiki, I think it's so extremely important that people understand the power of words. You cannot heal yourself without going into the past and drudging up the old stuff to forgive and learn from it. I use a list of good and bad words from Debbie Ford's book: The Dark Side of the Light Chasers. The idea is that any word that has any emotional response is one that you need to look at for resolution. This client has major issues with the words a family member used against her. We discussed how these words attach themselves to you and become part of you and can even hold you back from succeeding in life. It was powerful for her, and was necessary for her to forgive her family member in order for her to be whole.

Forgiveness is a huge part of Reiki 2 and necessary to heal the emotional part of our spirit.

Another powerful healing from words came with forgiveness as a client could not forgive her family member who had abused her. She had seen a therapist, and still the issue lingered. It was difficult to just listen to her story, I can't imagine living through it. We cried together and when she could finally put the emotion to the side, we talked. I asked her to ask herself just one question. "IF he truly UNDERSTOOD what he did to you, and how much it hurt YOU, do you think he would have done it?" This one question makes you think in a different way about your abuser. "IF the person had mental issues, he would not comprehend what he is doing. IF he had mental issues, you can understand the emotional capacity would not be the same as a normal person." She started to cry again. I continued, "then, you can forgive. This doesn't mean you have to ever communicate with him. But it will release his hurt from your heart. It starts to bring you back to wholeness, which you have been missing for a long time." It was as if the world was released from her shoulders. She now thought about this in a different light, and it made a shift in how she was able to move on. I believe we were all meant to work with each other at a certain point in our lives. THIS was the reason we were brought together. She could have learned Reiki from anyone, but she needed to get this one view point from me. I am so grateful I could help! This one client helped me realize the importance of this section of my Reiki class. I will always have this section in my class.

Reflection: It's important as Reiki Practitioners that we are able to handle ANY emotional issue that people are affected with in order to be whole again. If you can't forgive, how can you teach someone else to do the same? Healing is for the mind, body and spirit and is necessary for wholeness for one and all.

The very next Monday, I had another issue with words. I am noticing the things I need to learn come at me in threes. I taught others to forgive; now it was my turn. A person said that Reiki was "devil worship". At first it didn't bother me since I had heard this nonsense before, but as the night went on I became furious and so deeply wounded. I didn't know the person who said it personally but I sent an email to a group and told them what happened and that words can be hurtful. It set off a firestorm of emails, phone calls and visits from concerned people. The person came to apologize to me and I accepted the apology but that doesn't mean I had to be friends, or ever talk to the person again. A week later I still felt horrible. I wonder if this anger and depression about my work can be lifted. I couldn't understand why it was bothering me so much, and I didn't know how to get rid of the feeling.

When I spoke to the Denise Joy, the psychic at A Hand in Healing, she said this is a past life issue. So I meditated on it and found that in a past life my father had warned me not to do these healings. People would find out. It was evil and I'd be in trouble. But I said "it's good to help them be healthy." I couldn't hide the truth nor did I try. There was a black caldron I was in, and my father then taught me a lesson by setting it on fire as I cried out "It's good, I'm doing good. Why don't people understand this?" My own father wouldn't stick up for me as he was the priest in the town. I cried from the depths of my soul. I knew he didn't understand God's love, and this sadness filled my heart as I came out of the meditation. At least now I understood where the depression about the work came from, but I still needed to heal it.

March 24, 2012

Denise Joy did a past life regression with me with her channeled guides. At the time, we were in the middle of filming classes for the Nutmeg Public TV station, and decided to tape it. I was glad we did as I have viewed it many times since then, it is on You Tube here:(www.youtube. com/user/cherylcase1) and it was broadcast on Nutmeg TV. Denise told me that I had three or four past lives with this man who called my work "devil worship" and in every one; he was horrible, even killing me in one. (This was in my meditation!) I choose to come back in this lifetime with him again for his wife's sake. It helped me immensely in that it explained that I wouldn't have to ever deal with him again, and that I did the right thing by speaking up against injustice and ignorance. I should just give his issues to God to handle, and I needed to do a ceremony to put a close on this in my heart. It was so emotional for me, but I was so grateful to Denise for helping me through this in order to return to "normal" again. Before this session I had never considered that I may have past lives. She told me that I have been a midwife, physician, nurse, medicine woman and a healer for an entire village in Africa. This made me cry as I finally understood who my soul is, and that my love for my fellow human being is why I continue to heal people naturally.

Reflection: I never thought about the possibility that I had past lives. I never would have investigated the past lives had this not come to the surface. Consider it if you have something that is in your head and heart constantly. It is important to be able to understand why it is bothering you in order to release it. I can't say thank you enough to Denise Joy who was able to get me to understand this from another viewpoint. When you are stuck in your own story playing over and over in your head, it is best to seek help so you can move on.

March 29, 2012

I woke at 3 am and went into my son's vacant room. Archangel Raphael came and explained that just by being born I was healing my Mother. Mom was 41 years old when she had me and considered it a blessing as she didn't think she could get pregnant. He said I healed her heart and made her belief in God stronger. Always an instrument of HIS healing I was told. Then I thought of Dad, how just sitting and chatting would make him happy, no longer depressed. And having grandchildren at the time when he was very sick made it bearable for him. Part of the reason I am here is to heal all the people in my life that lied to me over the years. I never trusted them and eventually would get them to see that their dishonesty was why our relationship dissolved. I keep bringing those people into my life to show and teach them how wrong it is, and to heal them. Trust is such a HUGE moral value of mine, always has been, and this makes sense in my heart.

Reflection: Archangel Gabriel is the Truth Angel. I ask him to help me give the right words to those who need to learn the value of truth. It is disheartening to me to watch people leave my life because they are dishonest; however, it would hurt me more to keep them in my life. If you have hurt someone, and you know it, apologize so that you can move on. If you said something or did something to hurt others, the apology may or may not be accepted by the other person. Either way is ok, the important part is that you apologize to relieve the hurt in your heart. Learning the lesson is part of the human experience to make you a better person.

Fear is something that stops people in their tracks, and keeps them from moving forward in so many ways. I had always had a fear of driving in lots of traffic. Driving through Hartford, CT was terrifying; my hands would sweat as I gripped the steering wheel. No music could be on; I would have the air condition on high, even if it was winter. No one could talk and

I would barely go the speed limit. I always drove in the slow lane of this four lane highway. I knew this had to change. I had a session with a shaman who cleared the chakras with bells, rattles, and sage. The shaman learned the technique from Alberto Villoldo, author of the book: <u>Illumination: The Shamans Way of Healing.</u> At one point, I felt my stomach collapse and I really knew the fear was gone. I had a witness there who could see a huge, through the roof, black, gloppy scary thing standing by me. He didn't know what it was and I told him, "It's my fear." It was huge and consumed me. After it was over I was tired, but didn't think any more about it. Weeks later I did another drum circle with Sierra North and she released the fear again. A few weeks later, I had to drive through Hartford and I did it calmly, no sweating, and even had the radio on! THAT HAD NEVER HAPPENED BEFORE!!!! Yes, you have to be ready to release it, but once it is gone, the feeling is amazing! People go through their entire life holding on to emotions that are holding them back from life. Isn't it great that there are ways to change that naturally?? This personal experience helped me heal another client three years later who has the same exact issue. The fear is held in the sacral chakra, and the color orange is typically hated by the person going through this issue. Lots of work on fear needs to be explored to heal it!

Reflection: The opposite of fear is what is needed to heal it. All you need is LOVE. Reach out to God and feel the love. There were times when I had to have conversations in my head about driving through traffic. I needed to ask God to calm me with love so that I could get safely through Hartford. Then listen for advice, once I needed to go at a different time to avoid issues. Whatever message you get, do it if it the answer is from an unconditional loving source.

May 9, 2012

Shaman and Reiki Master Sierra North was videotaped for the Nutmeg TV series from A Hand in Healing today (also on Youtube). The healing for me alone was powerful as we worked on my second and third chakras. I was able to ask for the fear to leave and not return. Later in the evening I realized that the fear is from not being patient. The two are connected; with no patience the fear comes. There was an immediate shift once we did a meditation to the Wasac moon and were able to talk to the ascended masters. Jesus was there for me and said I need to learn patience, and as I do, the wisdom I get will be so great that I'll be able to teach it. I laughed since I've never heard of anyone teaching patience and for me to do it seems hilarious! I have been calmer since this drum circle, and that in itself is huge.

Four weeks later and I am still calm most of the time. Previously, I would feel people's emotions and it would affect me, now I am able to listen to the story, but am detached from the emotion. I am not sure I like this part of me, it's not something I intentionally wanted to change, and it seems weird after being that way my whole life.

Reflection: In the past, I looked at people who were not emotional as somehow lacking. Now I am grateful for this new ability to understand the emotion, empathize and get to the facts faster. Getting overwhelmed with emotion and not being able to move from it is certainly not healthy. I didn't think patience would bring this bonus of emotional balance but I am grateful beyond measure.

The AngelLink Series with Denise Joy started with the attunement to Seraph Rose Aura. Seraph Rose Aura is above the archangels and you need to be attuned to her before the Archangels Michael, Uriel, Gabriel and Raphael. Seraph Rose Aura connects you to Unconditional Love for yourself and others. Having had attunements before, I thought I had an understanding of how this would feel. When she put her hand in front of the heart chakra, I felt the energy go across my chest and down both arms, around to my back. The sensation was like a blanket of warm love, very comforting and soothing. Archangel Raphael is the angel of healing and the attunement is given in the hands. Two days after the class I gave a Reiki treatment and thought Archangel Raphael was there since the Reiki felt different, deeper into the person. The next treatment I did was the same, deep, and the physical therapist I worked on agreed it seemed to go deep into the tissue. Denise had said that those who are supposed to be healed by me will be. I'm now seeing people who either need deep healing or want to learn Reiki.

Reflection: When I first took Reiki, I remember being told that this was all you needed to heal. For the longest time, I didn't take any additional classes, as I truly felt I didn't need anything else. This one decision to take the Lightarian AngelLink classes enhanced my Reiki as I never would have imagined. The confidence I received has increased and the loving messages are clear, direct and accurate. The combination of Reiki while asking Seraph Rose Aura and the Archangels to assist is amazing!

They help speed up the process of healing while doing it in a loving and effortless way!

As powerful as receiving the attunements to the archangels were, I prefer giving them to others! There are times when I cry. The attunement feels like love and the emotion is simply bliss. To give the attunement and have clients express the same joy is so satisfying. I have found that this is very beneficial for people struggling with self-love. I gave a few attunements to people with amazing life changing results, and am sooooo grateful to Seraph Rose Aura for saving them. I am finding this especially helpful to young men who are finding it difficult to find their place in the world. If you have clients who are depressed for any reason, this is the best first step to take to get them to feel love for themselves.

June 7, 2012

Last night I attended the Uriel Angel Link with Denise Joy. As always it was an amazing class, but this particular gathering was very special as Archangel Uriel was very much present with us. Denise was able to channel his enlightened and love filled words. His message to us is: "to suspend all of our beliefs and welcome him with an open heart. Be ready and willing to have old beliefs fall to the way side and allow him to infuse you with new beliefs that will take you toward your creativity and beauty. The first beauty that will come to us is the beauty of ourselves and the perfection of who we are and where we are in our lives at this time. We are struggling with full self-expression and full self-acceptance. This will be the first old belief to fall away. We have both asked for this and that is why I (Archangel Uriel) am here to give it to you ... the support to move into your own personal beauty and your appreciation of that beauty. The fear of releasing your old beliefs will be taken from you. It will not stop the process. I will help you to transmute this fear of moving forward. You will expand and grow and take others with you. Your inner soul beauty connected to source will be a beacon for others to be drawn to you. They will see possibilities just from who you are. This is what you will bring to them. The possibilities are of letting go and falling into the beauty and joy. Being able and free to appreciate all that happens. What you will bring to others and what you will grow into is understanding that every step that you take ... every decision that you make is beautiful ... and accept it ... accept what you see as failures ... accept what you see as mistakes ... accept what you see as diminishing thoughts and see the beauty in them that they are all part of your path ... all interwoven. Please have appreciation that these experiences, beliefs and thoughts have brought you to where you are. All is perfection. I look forward to our connection. I look forward your softening in your fears that wrap around your hearts so that you will be able to gain all that is yours through this appreciation and viewing of the beauty of the world."

June 8, 2012

Denise Joy did a gallery reading for 4 people, which turned into public psychic sessions. One man had a ghost in his house, and Denise was able to confirm the name of the ghost, and verify the things that the ghost was doing....turning lights on and off, moving things, and making noises. The ghost was in the house for his grandson, but he is not afraid of him. A mother and daughter came together, and the mother wanted to know who her father was, as he was never confirmed. Denise told her that her Dad was who she thought he was, and everyone was crying. Before Denise could finish the mother's reading, Harriet showed up and Denise asked the mother if she knew her. The mother said she was here for her daughter, and yes she absolutely knew her. Denise then asked Harriet to wait so she could talk with another lady first. This next client talked about her grandmother's regret for all she had done to her. That the pain she has from it she is now holding in her elbow now and that's why it's not healing. She needs to be able to forgive them to heal, WOW! Now back to Harriet, who has been patiently waiting. Harriett is the daughter's 8th cousin, and is Harriett Beecher Stowe, author of Uncle Tom's Cabin! WE all just sat there in awe for a moment! She came to tell her cousin to write a book. The daughter said she has no experience or passion yet to do so, and Harriett was there to encourage her to get out there and find it! It was amazing to think Harriett would come to talk to her 8th cousin! She told her the world is at your fingertips! You have the internet, and can get on a plane, do it!

Reflection: Before purchasing A Hand in Healing, I had a psychic reading with Denise Joy. It was my very first reading, ever. I never believed in psychics before and have to say there are different levels of readers out there. She was able to give me specific info that convinced me she had a gift. People love going to psychic's to verify the intuitive side of them. All these people knew this information in their hearts, but having someone they never met verify it is the "blow me away" feeling we all got this day!

June 9, 2012

Barbara Hardie, author of <u>Creating Heaven on Earth- A Guide to Personal Ascension</u> came to discuss her book today. I had met her in November of 2011 at a Near Death Experience meeting with a friend and loved all she had to say. She got messages from her guides and Jesus for her book. When she signs the book and she writes a message from them to you. The message she wrote to me in November was "Blessings to you to pass on to your community." When I read that, I thought she must have meant it for someone else, as I had no community. But, by January 4, 2012 I did! A Hand in Healing became a possibility just after Thanksgiving! I gave her my book again today and asked her for a new message. "Congratulations, you are on your way to stardom! Continue to follow the light that your soul is shining on your path." "Wow", I thought "what a message!" Then, when thinking about it, I didn't like it. First of all, I don't understand stardom; I don't want to be a glittery Hollywood type star. Part of my Reiki 2 Practitioner class is to look at positive words that also bother you. I had to look in a mirror and try to figure out why "stardom" bothered me so much. I finally came to the conclusion that stardom could mean being an expert in something so that people would look at you in a different way, and I was comfortable with that, at last. It is so amazing to me how many times the things I have learned in the past come up again and again….until you learn the lesson!

Reflection: Getting comfortable with whom you are and what you do takes time, especially in this field! Trusting your experiences will bring you to a new comfort level, and the light begins to shine for all to see.

June 21, 2012

Mary Bach came to do an exercise where we meditated to find out past lives of others and made drawings of it. The two ladies that came made drawings of me, one in my back yard giving private information in a secretive style. Mary saw me in a sleek blue car, dressed in all red (of course!) being driven from an airport to a place where lots of people are waiting for me. Her message was that I got comfort in the car. It was a peaceful time to relax and read a script in the back seat. When I got home, I looked up cars from 1942, and there it was, a Cadillac! I do agree that being in my car now does give me comfort. On many days I get information and messages on the next step I need to take or guidance from my angels. God gives me direct messages in the car, which is why I always use the AA Michael prayer as I leave the driveway. I don't want to cause an accident while receiving messages on the road!

Reflection: If you are looking for messages, turn off the radio in your car. Look at your surroundings and take in the beauty of nature and start a conversation with your guides. Many times I would arrive at work and wonder how I got there as I was in deep conversation with my guides! Thank you Archangel Michael for watching out for me!

July 10, 2012

A client was diagnosed with nodes on her throat. I saw her twice, the first time her throat and neck were hot. The second time, I worked on her adrenals, throat and neck. Today, nothing on throat, all adrenals, and it was intense. My back was pounding which told me to stay there. I had to be on both sides at least half an hour. We asked for Archangel Michael and Raphael to come with Jesus. The pain got worse on my body, so I also asked Dr. Usui, and Mrs. Takata to come and help. It took a while, but the heat finally broke. The client said she felt my hand vibrating, as did I. For a while it was shaking internally so bad I felt it go up my arm. So I put one of my hands on her arm. She said she felt it up to her head and down her leg. I asked her if she noticed a difference in my Reiki, she said yes, it's deeper, so I guess I am on the right track. She goes back to the Dr. for another x-ray at the end of the month and she was not sure what to expect. She said "not a miracle." I looked at her and said "excuse me? I fully expect a miracle and so should you, as they happen every day, and YOU deserve one." We both started crying, I hugged her and I told her next time she comes we will do Reiki together. Some people lack the confidence to Reiki alone, and make the healing happen with faith. I hope to change that the next time she returns. People don't understand that YOU CAN heal yourself! She didn't return, and I am not sure if it was because she thought I was unrealistic or she lost faith in me. What I know for sure is that those who have faith in the Universe/God think from the heart, not the mind. This seems to be a huge difference when it comes to healing. You pray from the mind, but then something changes, and the prayers for healing come from the heart. I know this happens with me every time I give Reiki. The Reiki begins with a basic invocation I say every time, and then becomes heart centered where I genuinely ask God for whatever the client needs to heal. It is felt so deep within my heart, is so beautiful, that tears well up. As I give Reiki, I sense the person's soul, and wonder if this is what God sees in each of us. Beauty, innocence, love, and peace- it is in all of us. It doesn't matter what we look like, these qualities shine through. I have not shared this with my clients, yet when I do feel this, I know miracles happen.

In my Reiki sessions I see love EVERY time. It's hard to explain with words, but as the client relaxes and allows the healing Reiki energy to envelop their being, calm takes over. When I see their facial expressions mellow, their breathing slow and their body melts into the Reiki table, I know the healing is working. I see the absolute change in their demeanor as if there is not a care in the world. The love shines through. This is why I practice Reiki. All you need is LOVE.

July 10, 2012 Munay-Ki Rites 1-3

Sierra North comes to give Munay-Ki rites, founded by Alberto Villoldo. Munay-ki is a Quechua word that means "I Love You". There are 9 rites of initiation to become a person of wisdom and power who has accepted the stewardship for all creation. It originated from Hindus Valley to Americas by the first medicine man/woman that crossed the Barring Straits from Siberia during the glacial period 30,000 years ago. The Laika received grace through prayer, study of wisdom, teachings and discipline. Munay-Ki clears your luminous energy field of psychic sludge left by past life traumas. Past and future visions come as you raise your vibrations. DNA is upgraded, and can be influenced by who you are becoming. The final set of initiation downloads information to your DNA to create a new body that will age, heal and die differently. I'm hoping this is an upgrade as well! I am wondering if I need this or even if it should be changed? How do I know? Wasn't I born a perfect child of God? It's interesting since before I purchased this business 6 months ago, I had NO IDEA about these things or that they even existed. I never would have even gone looking for it, but now, because it's here, I am doing it. I'm hoping it's all beneficial, but I have no idea if it could be changing anything for the worse or before it should be? I wonder about that and want clarity on it, a knowing somewhere that

I don't have yet. The EARTH KEEPERS are to come when I'm ready, and I really need to know this stuff. I want more light for me and those I heal. The best would be to be protected from negative or low vibrational energies.

Nine of us pick a PI stone- a round stone with a hole in the middle. These stones are all in a bag, and I am last to pick. I say I want a red one, and am overly excited about it. I purposely wanted to be last to pick, and I got a Poppy Jasper, red, of course! This may have been needed to show others in the class that you really do get what you need!

Jasper, is a rain bringer, acts like adrenaline, waking up and energizing areas of the body that appear to be sleeping. It brings deep connection to life of the earth. Inspires positive, joyful attitude and gives energy to take creative action. It drives away evil spirits and protects against snake and spider bites. It enhances organizational abilities, relaxation and a sense of wholeness. It aligns chakras and balances yin-yang physical and emotional. Jasper brings protection during astral travel, helps animal allergies and eases stress. It is a powerful healing stone and exactly what I needed.

You wear the Pi stone and sleep with it for three months of the process and do a germination exercise with it daily. First you set up a sacred space, and hold the PI stone over fire which clears and activates the stone. Each time you hold the stone over the fire, then bring it to the respective area for the rite you are working on.

Rite One is the Healer's Rite which connects you to a lineage of luminous healers from the past to assist you in your personal transformation. Rite Two is the Bands of Power that are woven into your luminous energy field (LEF) for protection. And Rite Three is the Harmony Rite which is a transmission of the 7 Archetypes into the Chakras. Sierra has everyone drum as she gives each person the first rite, then starts again with the first person getting the second rite, and the same for the third rite. This session takes a long time, and everyone feels calm after it is complete.

I decide I need to journal what happens….keeping an open mind!

Day 1- after the first three rites were given I slept solid except waking up in the middle of the night with intense back pain. I acknowledged it was the Laika, as we were told they come at night. I asked that they be gentle and went back to sleep immediately.

Day 2- I woke at 2:30am with intense stomach pain, used the bathroom and went back to sleep, tired in the am, slight headache, but ok.

Day 3- woke at 2am with stomach pain, got up and did the Munay-Ki rites. Tired in AM, got to work late, but noticed my face seemed smoother.

Day 4-For the first time ever, I did 2 Reiki treatments, 2 hours apart. I was fine for both, then slept 1.5 hours when I got home, left ear was tingly. Had lots of energy when I got up!

Day 5- not sure what's going on...took off the PI stone for an hour, and I got dizzy on the right side, so I put it back on. Strange sensations, but feeling grounded.

Day 7- I woke up hot, and am not sure if this is the Munay-Ki or menopausal hot flashes! I am drinking so much water, can't get enough! I'm noticing the Reiki I am doing seemed more intense. Yesterday, I has a lady with adrenal issues. I used selenite, amethyst, aegrine and merlin crystal to break up the energy. I was in one spot for at least 15 minutes.... deep healing happening!

Day 8- woke up at 3:03am wide awake! No pain, just up! At drum circle today, Sierra reminded us to cut energies from people we worked on.

The other people in the group experienced similar wakening's in the night, the need for more water and everyone was taking better care of their bodies....well, that was enough for all of us to want to keep going!

Reflection: I later notice that when I get sick, it moves through me quickly and is not as intense as it is for the rest of the family.

August 3, 2012

Denise Joy's Reiki session started out being a basic session. I asked my guides and Denise's guides and angels to come and help remove any negative issues from her. I used the merlin generator on her crown chakra and the crystal was tingling in my hands as soon as I put it near her, removing the negative energy. I then asked AA Raphael to bring his green healing light to fill all the spaces that were cleared. Denise started having twitching movements in her feet and legs and felt like she wanted to leave her body. Luckily, I had used one color stone for each of the corresponding chakras and a black tourmaline to ground her. It was only at the end when she wanted to take the stones off of her. As I was at her head giving her Reiki, she wanted to touch my hand to see where my thumb was, as she felt pressure in another area. She said it felt like AA Raphael was putting a crystal – 6 inches or so, into her brain. When she asked him what he was doing, the reply was "getting her brain ready to connect directly with God."

When it happens she will know it and it will be instant and monumental. I said "wow" and felt like crying but told myself this is a professional session, hold it together. The session was only 45 minutes, but incredibly powerful for her. When the client is ready, they get what they need! Denise said she's always been connected to Spirit yet knew she also needs to be connected physically in her body and this brought it into her cells! She knew now what she needed to heal her body to go on to bigger work! I was honored to have been able to give her what she needed to grow today!

Reflection: The merlin generator is six faces coming to a pyramid point. The point needs to be pointy not broken. This stone clears all the chakras. The one I used was so big I had to use two hands to hold it. Many people will tell you that the size is not important. I do notice that the larger the stone is or the amount of stones I have is important. I always ask my guides:" Is this is enough?" "Is there another I need?" Listen for the answers and trust it.

Sometimes I will ask my pendulum for additional information. Using a pendulum is easy. To choose one, hold it over one hand and ask it to show you a "yes" answer. It will move in one direction, typically mine goes clockwise, almost from one side of my palm to the other, in a large circle. Then say thank you before asking it to show you a "no" answer. Again, it will move in a different direction. Then ask it if your name is _____. It should say yes. You can then ask it another question that you know is a no answer. When it can do all of that, then you have found your pendulum! That is how you know it is yours and you should purchase it. If it is not moving, or moving in a small circle, it's not the right one for you. I have several that I use for different reasons. I use a selenite pendulum to open chakras, another which is red jasper to check chakras, a metal one for water dowsing, and the lilac lepidolite that I use for business questions.

August 14, 2012

Denise Joy's reading brought one man into a connection with his Dad. The man said his Dad never told him he loved him, and tonight his Dad apologized and told him how proud he is of him. We were all in tears; his Dad said that on the other side, you are the evaluator of your life. He is sooooo sorry he didn't do a better job. Later the man told me how he is now doing the same thing to his own son. He said that they are sooooo distant and he only says "HI" to him. I suggested he add "I LOVE YOU" to let his son know that he supports him. It was a lightbulb moment for him. No one wants to live with this after death, wishing they could do it over. THIS IS THE STUFF I LOVE! A Hand in Healing is reaching people, one at a time!

August 18, 2012

I was sooooo excited to have Kirlian photography of my aura done! You sit in a chair and put your hands on a device while someone takes your picture with a Polaroid type camera. In a few minutes the picture is done! As the picture is developing, a description of your aura colors prints on paper for you to read. Mine was mostly a gorgeous yellow, meaning creative! The lady who took the pictures had been to Paris, France on a mission, although she didn't know until she got there. Her guides told her to go and she ended up at the Chapel of the Miraculous Medal. She has now given out over 650 medals of the Virgin Mary! She gave our group as many as you wanted today. I decided to look up the chapel and read about it. There's a ton of medals you can buy and when I saw one in particular, it minded me of the one I got from my Grandmother years ago. I ran to find it, and sure enough it's the one! Mine is silver and mother of pearl under the Virgin Mary medal. I've used it in stressful times and pray to her when I need to be calm, she helps me EVERY time. I now wear this medal daily, without fail.

Reflection: It's interesting that I knew about this medal before, yet ignored it in my jewelry box. I suggest you search your jewelry boxes to see what you may have that could benefit you today!

August 21, 2012

Munay Ki Rites 4 to 6 with Sierra North....

Rite Four is the Seer's Rite where pathways of light connect the visual cortex with the third eye and heart chakra. This awakens the inner seer and your ability to perceive the invisible world of energy and Spirit. Rite Five is the Daykeeper's Rite which connects you to a lineage of master healers from ancient times. And Rite Six is the Wisdomkeeper's Rite which connects to a lineage of luminous beings from the past and the future.

We did a journey after and I asked to be given more power to heal. Some participants don't ask for anything, they just keep an open mind. I always ask for a specific healing, today I want my sinuses healed. I can't remember ever being able to smell. Growing up with a parent smoking three packs of cigarettes a day may have something to do with this issue. As I sat there, I received more Reiki in my hands than I remember getting in a very long time. I thank the stone altars for their power and now have a need to find out more about the Stonehenge. This must be why Reiki students go there on a yearly journey. I was so energized that I didn't go to bed until 12:30am that night and was totally energized the next day as well!

Reflection: In the year 2016, I read a book that suggests Jesus went to Stonehenge! This is something to add onto my bucket list now!

August 28, 2012

I woke in the middle of the night as I heard voices talking. I was in such a deep sleep that I couldn't hear what they were saying. I started thinking why hasn't my husband turned off the alarm yet. As I started to wake up more fully, I noticed that it was only 3am, and that it wasn't the alarm, but probably the Laika! Now I was annoyed that I couldn't hear what they were saying! I woke up dizzy and tired and had a third eye headache. Went back to bed and got up a few hours later, ate, went back to bed, got up for lunch, back to bed. I was sooooo incredibly tired. Finally, I got up at 5:30pm and wasn't as tired, and the dizziness was finally gone. I asked the Laika to continue to heal my third eye and left eye. I felt a type of laser in back of the left eye. As I was born with ascendant Aries I am aware of sinus and eye problems and am hoping the Laika were able to do something important here!

August 30, 2012

I got some relief today, only had a headache, the third eye pain was only in the morning. I came home to my husband making dinner, steak and chicken on the grill. I commented that it SMELLED good. I didn't pay attention to it, later while doing dishes I could still SMELL the steak, and then BAM hit me....I CAN SMELL!!! This has been a lifetime ailment, so I pinch myself to be sure I am not dreaming. Then I thought about my day....I had commented on how good an orange smelled as a co-worker was peeling it at her desk. And my boss had on perfume…which she said she wears daily- that I never smelled before today. Eleven years I didn't smell it! I ran around the house smelling everything! Soaps, lotions, perfumes in shampoos and candles! I was so excited I didn't want to go to sleep for fear the sense of smell would go away. This was overwhelmingly wonderful! I was on smell overload! How do you stop it? How do you clear the smells? This was hilarious, yet amazing stuff! There was no one else I could credit but the Laika! THANK YOU! It is days like this that I think, why aren't more people experiencing these classes?

September 9, 2012

I notice that my sense of taste has also changed, of course. Things seem strong to me now, where before I would cook, for example, with eight cloves of garlic just to taste it and now it's way too much! The onions on the potato were hot tonight, and I feel my taste buds have kicked in! YIPEE!

Reflection: I don't know how long this lasted, but my sense of smell comes and goes now. I can't say I actively worked on giving myself Reiki here or I believe I would heal it. When you grow up with no sense of smell, it doesn't seem like something I needed. It did, however, enhance my faith in healing with the Munay-Ki rites.

September 16, 2012

The first time I gave attunements to three people in one class! There was so much energy expended through me, my heart was racing when I sat down and again later that night. I had to ask all "A TEAM" (angel team) to come and help me. This Reiki 2 class was focused on forgiveness. One client had just come out of a depression two days before class. She was in need of this class to deal with forgiveness of herself for getting sick and not being able to go on vacation with her family. The second client needed forgiveness of self for being the one who took away another's husband, in her words. I had to remind her that their relationship must not have been good in order for this to happen. She agreed and found comfort in those words. The third client needed to forgive herself for not being able to totally help her sister. I needed to remind her it's not totally her job to be in control of her sister's health. Sometimes people have contracts with God, and although we don't like it, we must understand it is not our life path, and not in our control to fix or change it.

Reflection: You always get what you need for energy of the Reiki class. Before class I was worried as a lot of energy is needed to pass attunements. Remember, you always get what you need! I would not personally do more than three Practitioners for the four hour time allotted because I give two attunements per person for a four hour class. Reiki 1 and Reiki 2 classes receive a total of four attunements per degree. The attunements are what increase your energy vibration and are the main "event" of the class. I tell the Practitioners this is what makes the class, it is your time to connect with spirit, meditate and listen for answers. Once I am done giving the attunements, I sit down and wait for the Practitioners to determine when it's complete by opening their eyes. Some people only give one attunement, and the Practitioners' energy is not the same as someone who has had four attunements. This one thing can make a Practitioner give up Reiki because they don't understand "what's the big deal." It takes my Reiki Master Practitioners longer (typically a year) to go through Reiki Master class and be able to pass four attunements on one person. The Master must have built up the energy within them to be able to do this for others. There are so many changes to the Master within the year, ranging from their own emotional, physical and spiritual beliefs. I know when they graduate that they are able to heal emotional issues as well as physical issues. The differences between Masters who have concentrated on this for a year versus an eight hour class are huge! This is why Usui Reiki is called a healing art!

Reflection: I noticed that although it was easy for me to tell someone else it is not in our control to fix or change others life paths, it is not so easy for me to do! Depending on the relationship you have with the individual, and how close you are to the person, will determine your emotional investment. The closer you are to the person, the harder it is to accept they have their own will. Your connection to them grows your hearts closer, and of course you don't want to lose that connection. It will be years before I get this lesson wholeheartedly.

Back in February I made a wand. The instructor of the class said we could use sticks from our yard, so I used sticks from our Red Twig Dogwood since I just LOVE the color red! I used red, black, clear and purple beads on it and put it on a shelf and left it there. I never felt the need to use it, and then one day in August, I decided it needed two small double terminated crystals, one on each end. I wrapped them with silver wire and the curve in the middle of the wand made me hold it so that it felt like it needed to pour energy. I tried it on one person in the store at the time and poured energy into her crown chakra. She said it was very powerful, felt like liquid gold, very hot! She felt it as I went down each chakra. When I put it down, my arms were very heavy from the energy.

Tonight I did a cellular memory meditation from the book: A Torch in Daylight by Karyn Mitchell with the three Reiki 2 Practitioners. It's about telling your cells you are healthy, whole, well and complete. The mediation itself is enough but I decided this is where I'd use the wand. Using no Reiki, I held the wand at the crown chakra, did all the symbols and said aloud that they were healthy, whole, well and complete as the energy went down from crown to root chakra and then to Mother Earth. Then I returned energy back up through all the chakra's to the 12th chakra and asked the energy to continue to flow to heal all cells, make them healthy, whole, well and complete. They loved it! Again, my arms were so heavy and tired, what a wand! Intention is a big part of everything you do. If you intend to heal, you will. Put your whole heart and soul into it, and use powerful words. The Universe will deliver. This wand has a power of its own and I use it with Reiki class during meditations.

Reflection: Sometimes you start something and put it to the side because you don't know what to do with it. I have done this several times with pieces of furniture or something that caught my eye that I just had to have, but wasn't sure why. Sometimes it is several years later when you figure out why you really needed that piece. Follow your heart, as these items may be hard to find at the time when you want to use it. I use the terminology "healthy, whole, well and complete" when asking Archangels Michael and Raphael to heal someone.

September 19, 2012

Munay Ki Rites 7-9 with Sierra North

The seventh rite is the Earth Keeper which connects you to lineage of archangels that are guardians of our galaxy. We can call them to bring healing and balance to any situation. They help you dream the world into being. I asked Sierra why the world was still so bad, if this were possible. She said, "not enough people are using them". I joked that I'm calling President Obama and getting him to the next class! I was first to be attuned for all these rites tonight. I did mentally ask to be first but was still surprised when it happened! I notice more and more that the requests I have typically happen now! At each attunement I asked that I be connected with whatever was for my highest and greatest good.

The eighth rite is the Starkeeper rite, Sierra's favorite, which anchors you safely to time after the great change of 2012. The ninth rite is the Creator rite, which awakens the God light within you and you acquire stewardship for all creation. You can ask for the role you are in creation to effect positive change. During the attunement, I asked for connection to Jesus and believe I got him and God. When I got up from the floor, Sierra always bows her head to you and I said thank you and started to cry. She hugged me. I was the only one that got a hug directly after the last rite, and it was special. Later, before she left she told me the vibration was extremely high for me. She went to put the attunement in my 3rd eye and her hand ended up on my head. This took a while for her to complete and she said she couldn't move her hand. I was wondering what was taking so long! She had to ask a few times if she was done before she could move. Her hand felt very heavy on my head, weighty, pushing down. As it was there, I was thinking, wow, this is taking a while, and that she really should be hurrying as she had 9 more people to attune. Not to mention, everyone was drumming during this time, and as the shop owner, I never want any more attention than anyone else. When she was done, I felt light headed and tired. I asked the Laika to work on me tonight! I am wondering what changes will come because of this class. The weird part is that since you can't see what you would have been like without it, it's hard to ever really know! There is always something that comes up to link the class info to the experience....so amazing!

Reflection: Any time people take Reiki with me I let them know the attunements are the most important part of the class. I tell them after I am done giving the attunements I will sit down and wait for them to open their eyes. I don't care how long it takes as some very important work is happening at this time. The guides are working on you or you are experiencing eye opening revelations. I encourage them to write down what they experienced before talking about it for fear of losing any important information. So if you are getting a Munay-Ki attunement or a Reiki attunement, or any other kind, take the time to let the experience happen. Enjoy the journey!

October 4, 2012

I started the Lightarian Institute Maitreya Ray program. This is the empowerment ray that balances the male/female and connects with these ascended masters:

Babji- Beauty

Buddha- Compassion

El Morya- Power

Hilarion- Love

Krishna – Will

Kuthemi- Loyalty

Lady Mary- Justice

Lady Nada- Imagination

Lanto-Joy

Sananda- Purity

Serapis Bey- Curiosity

St. Germain- Courage

The attunement felt tingly all over and was for the acceleration of spiritual process of empowerment, clearing, healing, activation and manifestation. I felt empowered by GOD a few times already. It's as if the words of logic come out of my mouth without me even needing to think about it, it just happens. I had to discuss the lease agreement with my landlord and he began by saying he wasn't certain if he'd agree to the changes I'd made to the contract (which I had reviewed by a lawyer, so I knew they were abiding by CT law). Now normally, my heart would be racing since he is in control of this situation, not me. Instead, I was able to put the emotion aside and talk business calmly and rationally and got him to agree to all the changes....I was amazed and thought that this is the true meaning of power!

Reflection: When I got the lease agreement from my landlord, the wording was old, and some of the conditions were not to my benefit. This agreement was over 20 pages and he had used it with all his clients over the years. I reworded the parts I didn't like and Reiki'd it before I gave it back to him. He called me the next day and told me he didn't think he'd be able to lease to me with all of these changes. Normally I would been very upset and gotten very emotional. Instead, I remembered I gave the agreement Reiki before giving it back to him and said, "Let's review it together if you have a moment." He agreed and by going over it line by line and explaining why I thought the wording needed to be changed, it worked to my advantage. My intention was to get the lease under my terms, if it was meant to be, and clearly it was at that time!

October 9, 2012

I gave Reiki to a client who had heart problems, clogged arteries in legs, and back issues. It was a lot to work on and she only wanted a half hour. This is so difficult for me, as I wish I could have done more. My ego needs to stay out of it, and just give what she is willing to receive. This is the down side of being a Reiki Master; you want to fix everything for everyone. NOW!

October 10, 2012

I had a BioMat session for the first time! The mats are filed with amethyst and black tourmaline. You plug it in and on the lowest setting it was warm and I really felt it on my lower back. Two days later, major detox happened, I slept a lot, and the back pain I was having since the last Munay-Ki class was finally gone! Intense clearing was going on, so I started praying that it now clear on the spiritual level instead, to give me a break physically.

Reflection: A lot of ascension symptoms show up and can be a distraction during the day. I have to make it a point to ask that physical interruptions are kept to a minimum during working hours. Ascension symptoms can be: headaches, achy body, lots of energy to feeling sad, waking up at 3 am, heightened sensitivities and changing relationships to name a few.

On the same day, a person told me about a Usui Reiki Teacher who had her students practice on a CPR dummy! I get so angry when I hear this information! HOW can anyone feel energy on a PLASTIC dummy??? How can the dummy give you feedback??? The students learning thought it was odd, yet because there was a teacher telling them to do this, they practiced on a CPR dummy! This infuriates me!! Each time I hear about this, I instantly offer the person a free new class....I feel the obligation to try and correct the wrong that the Reiki Teacher did to the Practitioner. In my opinion, this is why Reiki is getting a bad reputation and people have no confidence in it. People pay a considerable amount of money, and then to get that kind of instruction is demeaning to the art of Reiki.

Reflection: Be sure to do your homework before you give your money to someone. Be sure to ask your Reiki Master these basic questions: Do you belong to any certification boards? Do you have insurance? Do you have testimonials? May I see your Reiki lineage? How long have you been teaching? May I call one of your students? There is a lot of discussion on the value of the Reiki lineage. Some say if it all comes from Dr. Usui, what difference does it make? I like the idea of knowing where it came from as a form of a family tree. This also lends credibility to the instructor versus thinking the person said they had it, but was making it up. The price you pay may change depending on how many attunements are given. I highly recommend four, as your energy is so much stronger!

December 27, 2012

Reiki 2 class for 2 Practitioners, WOW! The last two attunements didn't feel powerful to me, yet their experience was great! One said he felt the last attunement go down from his crown chakra, down each chakra to the root and then travel back up. He said it felt like a volcano! I explained that's exactly how I envision the attunement happening! I actually feel the energy go down into each chakra and wait until I know it went all the way down and then back up. At times when I know it's stuck, I envision it expanding with the corresponding chakra color light until the energy moves. We worked on each other and he had a block around his heart chakra. It felt like a wall, hard, and not moving. The other Practitioner and I worked on his heart chakra and I asked Seraph Rose Aura to come help. Within minutes, it became soft and he was crying. He said he felt intense love and was so grateful to us. He said, "NOW I understand why people cry" The moment was so empowering for him. I can't type the appropriate words to express the kindness and life changing moment this was for him. It is so emotionally satisfying to witness this huge change in someone. I never realized why some people never showed emotion. Maybe their heart chakras are blocked. This was a big learning lesson here for all of us! I believe this also had a lot to do with his heart being ready to be opened as well. It would not happen before, during Reiki 1 class. He had to allow it in!

Reflection: This client did a lot of personal healing since the very first time I gave him Reiki. I knew back then that he wanted to heal himself as this was the first time I played Reiki ping pong. Reiki ping pong happens when you give Reiki in one spot and the spot needing Reiki moves to another spot. When you go to the new spot and Reiki it, it moves back to the first spot, and this happens over and over again. When I finally understood what was happening I told him I couldn't heal it, he needed to be able to do it himself. He totally agreed and took Reiki 1.

Reflection: There are moments you never forget, this was one of mine! To be able to provide this kind of change in someone's life is what makes it all worthwhile! This is the soul healing I wanted to be able to provide, and it's working! I LOVE USUI REIKI!

January 1, 2013

It's a new year and I am still trying to figure out why Reiki is not more popular here in CT. In CA, AZ, and out West in general, there are natural healing places all over…yet here, not so common! People are certainly seeing the results with Reiki and the other classes. We are trying to now show it on Nutmeg TV, to get people to understand that there is nothing to be afraid of; spirituality is within all of us! How you experience it is different for each person, yet there is a way for everyone!

January 2, 2013

Sierra North thinks I have an attachment, she is sending me a healing meditation CD and tells me to do it as many times as possible in a week. She said a lot of people have them and they are attracted to us because of the light we are sending out to others. She said this happens when we are ready to handle it, and although I believe her, I am hoping I am ready! Two days later, I woke in the middle of the night thinking I had an attachment on my left ovary! I used Reiki and kept telling it that it was time to leave. I was thankful for the lesson but it needed to leave now. I finally got it to leave by asking Archangel Michael to remove it with his "vacuum" and then asked Archangel Raphael to replace the negative cells with love, healthy cells and light.

Reflection: All Reiki Masters should have someone they can turn to for help. Just because you are a master doesn't mean you can handle it all, or have seen it all. The Reiki community is large enough to find the help you need, use it!

January 4, 2013

The one year anniversary of A Hand in Healing!!! Although this should have been a joyous event, only one person came in to chat. Not realizing it was the year anniversary, my client brought me a chocolate frosty! MY FAVORITE!! We ended up talking for three hours and it felt like 10 minutes. This happens when you are on the same path spiritually! Thank you dear friend!

January 8, 2013

We have a Theta healing class with nine people. Everyone gave the instructor something they wanted healed. The instructor made a list on a pad and in about 10 minutes he was done. Everyone in the class felt something, tingly hands, lighter or just peace. I wanted the block gone; he called it "life in the way of success". I didn't like the name of it, and then while meditating, I discovered he was right. I felt my son's life at college was more important than my success. I felt my time had to wait. NOW that I am aware of it, and it is gone, I believe both can reside side by side. He said he removed the fear that was at the top of the building corner roof. He also mentioned that you can train a building to have certain characteristics. For the business I asked that there is success for all the instructors, trust of the customers, and a beacon of light for all. Everyone looked calmer when they left than when they came in.

Reflection: Before you move to a new office or home you should try to get some alone time in the space and feel the energy of it. Before we moved into our home, I just sat in the middle of one room and "talked" to my house. I first asked that it protect our family, that it be a place to keep us all calm, healthy and promote our individual interests. I then asked the house its name. This took time to tune into, but then Jethro announced himself. I asked three times if Jethro was correct, as it is not a common name. He said "yes, I am fun, strong and very protective," just what I wanted! Every day as I leave for work I ask Jethro to be here for us when we get back from the day's activities, and thank him for all he does for us. Think about your home and work spaces and be grateful for all that they provide you. By continually thanking these spaces, you build up a vibration of love and sacredness in them. This is why when you come home from a day of hard work, you relax at home. Now think about how you feel about going to work on Monday morning. If you give thanks to your work, for the paycheck it brings to allow you to provide for your needs and the love of your profession, it too will feel sacred. Continually add Reiki symbols to the entire building, individual rooms, even your computer! When energy feels stale, use sage, a crystal bell or a clearing spritz to reinvigorate the healing energy and eliminate the negative energy!

January 8, 2013

My mother has shingles and is in excruciating pain. I have never seen her will decline so quickly. She actually asked to die. In the middle of sleep, I suddenly wake up with pain in my left leg close to the top. I didn't get it that it was my mother coming to me until it went to my left ovary. I then asked if this pain was my own, and the answer was no. I then asked if it was my mother and I feel her silly grin looking at me. Is this the attachment Sierra talked about earlier on January 2? I was so angry that she was back and told her to go to Jesus and God and leave me alone. She told me she was ready to die and wanted me to go with her. I said I love you, but I am sorry I don't want to die with you and will not give you my energy. I said "I forgive you" and asked her to go to the light. I started cutting cords with my selenite stick, over and over, again and again, for a good amount of time. I was exhausted the next day and tired of her taking my energy. I talked to another healer about this and was told that in a past life we were nuns together, I laughed. Mom always calls me a nun, saying I am too good. He told me that she didn't believe she could get what she wanted from the other nuns, that she needed me. Last time I went to see her with the shingles she actually said "You're the only one who can heal me." WOW, this rang so true to me, I was shaking. The healer told me not to send her energy as this encourages her to keep returning to me. I finally understood why I've felt this way my WHOLE ENTIRE LIFE. Now new emotions are coming up for me, anger that this is why she had me in the first place. Did she think she could just take my energy any time she needed it? This is the first time I realize the connection between my menstrual cycles being so out of whack and her energy increase. There is a connection here, weird, but something I need to monitor more closely. This is not unconditional love, and is everything I am working against professionally.

Reflection: It felt unnatural to not want to heal my mother. Of course I wanted her well. But with her in this state of mind, wanting to die, I couldn't heal her and I certainly wasn't ready to die. This is one of those moments

I couldn't believe this is happening. My mother is ALIVE and yet able to come to me and discuss dying and me going with her! Part of me wanted to discuss this with her in a live conversation, and the other part knew not to go there.

January 10, 2013

At home that night I removed my mother's jewelry from the bedroom. She had given me her belongings to hold while she had shingles. I also removed the blankets and clothing from under our bed and took off her wedding ring and my Grandmother's wedding ring too. I called AA Michael to protect me and keep my mother's spirit off the property. I placed rose quartz for love and black tourmaline for protection in the four corners of the bedroom, and asked this grid of protection to keep me safe from any negative or low vibrational energy. Again, in the middle of the night, God and Jesus came with Mom, each holding one of her arms like she was being held back. I was at least blessed that she is not by herself coming to me with her angry energy. I told her again, using the Hoponopono prayer: I love you, I am sorry I can't go with you, please forgive me, and thank you. She was sad. I told her, "Dad and your sisters and family are waiting for you." She didn't say anything, God and Jesus turned her around and she left peacefully. I don't know how much moving her stuff out of my room helped, but I felt better that it was gone. Part of me is so sad that I have to do this with my own mother. I had NEVER heard of attachments with people who are still alive, and yet I need to separate from her for my own good. She has some type of strong hold over me that I can't seem to keep off of me. It is exhausting to be wary of sleeping every night. I am not getting enough solid sleep now.

Reflection: Material things hold energy. Look around your home, under your bed, in closets, basements, attics and garages. If you have no use for the item, you have not used it in over a year, or looking at it doesn't make you happy, donate it to someone who will use it. If it is broken and you don't know when or how you will fix it, remove it from your home. I have done several house clearings for people with a crystal bell and without knowing the people can tell them which items have negative energy. I remove the negative energy with Reiki and then replace it with loving energy. Then it can be donated with the intention that the rightful owner finds it.

January 11, 2013

A client asks me to do space clearing at her home. I have never been there before and bring my crystal bell and sage with me. The home is huge, and has lots of windows and skylights. I start in the east on the lowest level of the home and work my way up floor by floor. I stop in front of a brand new grandfather clock. It's surprising to me that it needs to be cleared, and the owner tells me this story after we are done clearing the house. When the clock was delivered, the husband was home and instructed the delivery men to put it on a certain wall. When the wife arrived, she told her husband that it was on the wrong wall and asked him to move it. Her husband was not happy about it and pushed and shoved the new clock against the wall all while swearing about having to move it. This energy was now in the clock! Negative energy comes in various forms: from sickness, arguments, neglect, hatred thoughts, all of which need to be cleared. I clear my house at least seasonally unless something happens in between that require it to be done on a more frequent basis. Also, any time I bring something into the house from any place else, I clear it. Be especially careful with items that were previously used from tag sales and antique stores.

January 13, 2013

Yesterday I read for three hours about Theta healing. Today I learned about Storyless Distance Healing, a technique from Leigh Russell, JR. and I feel it is basically the same thing as Theta, and faster. I was able to send healing to someone and she said her fever was breaking. I fully expect her to go to work tomorrow. She felt so much better.

January 20, 2013

A client called someone else for a Reiki class and the person never called her back. She emailed person number two and never heard back. She googled and found me! I was very happy as I need people to find me, I am not advertising a lot and have asked St. Germaine for help finding the perfect customers for me! She had breast cancer and wants to help those with cancer now. She had a great first Reiki attunement, she cried as she said she saw the white light, and saw herself in the snow with a wolf. All good signs to her! The second attunement was good, but she said different from the first. I explained each one is different. She later commented that she was glad she was alone with me. I explained everything happens for a reason. She said it was beautiful!

January 21, 2013

A Despachio Class with Sierra North. Five of us participated in a ceremony of blessings to Mother Earth and blessings for each other and our families. Sierra brought snake skin, flowers, red roses, salt, red pepper, chili powder, sugar, cinnamon, lavender, tobacco, seeds, blessed water, bay leaves, pine cones and feathers. We each started with three bay leaves. We held them with two hands and each leaf gets one blessing or wish. One is for Mother Earth for peace, healing and love. I used one for blessings of AHIH and one for my family. You approach the table covered with many layers of tissue paper and place them in the center, making a circle. Then each person takes a turn going to get one of the other ingredients based on what you want to add to your blessings. It's is done with intention, prayer and contemplation. I picked red roses for love, and it is AHIH symbol. I couldn't rip the leaves off the roses. I remembered my favorite quote by author Anais Nin: "And the day came when the risk it took to blossom was greater than the risk to remain tight in a bud." I opened the rest of the rose, and placed it on the seashell in the center. I picked candy stars to bring us all to a higher place, lavender for healing anyone who comes into AHIH, tobacco for protection, sugar to realize the sweetness of life, seeds for continued growth of all of us learning, chili peppers to spice things up and a shell for each family member. I put a swan feather over the rose in the middle to bring in the female compassion energy into AHIH. The picture of the end product was gorgeous; everyone added what they needed in their life. It was snowing outside and made the whole process very peaceful. When it was done, Sierra wrapped it up with ribbons and a rose. We then blessed each other with this package by placing it on each other's heads and wiping it over our arms, front and back of each of us. We all felt the love, intentions and prayers that were contained within. We all went outside and burned it to send the blessings to the Universe. It was magical to watch the smoke gently rise to the heavens.

January 26, 2013

I moved more stuff to the clearance area today. It made room for a Reiki shelf! I don't know why it took so long to do that, as I want the place to be known for Reiki! More people are starting to find us, I am grateful to St Germaine who had a hand in moving this along! Manifestation Ray is kicking in!

January 30, 2013

Drum circle tonight was amazing for me! While the ladies were drumming for me I saw the light like when I had my first Reiki attunement! Sierra North said I let go of something huge, but neither or us knew what it was. She was using a wood block and finally ended up throwing it to the floor to release the "thing". When I heard it hit the floor I was grateful to her for getting rid of it. Another drummer used the sea turtle drum. It told her I am like the turtle, and need to know that my baby, AHIH is ok. That like laying eggs in sand, I can then walk away and they will be fine. I think that's my cue that I can concentrate on Reiki now. All the others in the group are on their way! Also, that although I always say it's not me bringing in the Reiki energy, that it's God bringing in what I need, the conduit has to be clear. I have done the work and the energy that comes through me is high because of the work I do there. I need to charge more for it, to put value on it. Also Sierra said that the last time I gave her Reiki, she knows my energy is pure, because she constantly checks when people offer to Reiki her, and she blocks any that is not clear. She said my energy is hugely different. That means a lot to me, coming from her. I value her talents and gifts. We are all blessed to be together!

Reflection: I keep the prices low for Reiki sessions as it is not currently covered by insurance. I want Reiki to be available to everyone and my hope is by keeping it low, we are sharing the light with more people.

February 2, 2013

I met a woman who was an emergency responder to the September 11 attack in New York. She brought Reiki to a lot of people there and to the responders at Sandy Hook School in CT. With a team of 14, including two military men, they stayed at the school for two weeks helping faculty and staff transition back to school. She is an amazing woman, and I am so grateful to her for her service!

Reflection: I didn't realize that Reiki was used in official capacities in emergencies, as this was the first time I heard about it. I will have to look into this more to see where A Hand in Healing may be of assistance. We all need to do our part to heal in any way we can help. All Reiki Practitioners should do their part to give back in their own special way.

February 6, 2013

Source Ray Lightarian Class connects us to God and eight other ascended masters!

Universal Source – Will
Maitrea- Power
Buddha- Compassion
El Morya- Power
Hilarion- Love
Krishna- Will
Kuthumi- Loyalty
Lady Mary- Justice
Lady Nada- Imagination
Lanto- Joy
Sananda- Purity
Serapis Bey- Curiosity
St Germaine- Courage

The attunement started at the crown chakra went to the back of head, chest, then down to root chakra. It was hot at the crown and almost non-existent for me at the root.

Reflection: Although this is a long list of deity attunements, I can honestly say you get what you need. Some of them I never call on, however, once you are attuned with them, they work silently in the background. The important part of getting the attunements is to trust the person who is giving them to you. The person giving you the attunement should have a loving heart.

Reiki is a process of bringing you what you need when you need it. As your vibrational energy changes, higher energy frequencies are brought to you. These additional attunements help increase the amount of Reiki energy you can provide as well! As you are able to handle higher vibrational energies, more clients who need this find your services. My clients change as I do, and you will notice this as well!

February 22, 2013

A Reiki 1 Practitioner broke down in tears after I asked her what name she wanted me to write on her certificate. She hates the formality of her legal first name, and really likes the nickname of it better. She gave up the nickname years ago to become a third option, which she thinks is more "likeable and authoritative." She will be using a new name for a different job and wants to decide before taking that on. She has issues with voicing her opinion because she wants to be known as nice. Very interesting since her new job uses her voice. Six months pass before I contact her again about the blank certificate I have waiting for her. She decided to go with the third option…likeable and authoritative. Several years ago I knew another lady that hated the name everyone called her. This came up because I needed her legal signature and I thought it was beautiful. She said "yes, it is, but no one calls me that, ever". So I said "why don't you change that?" She thought about it a second and said, "How?" I told her any time someone calls you by the name you don't like, simply put out your hand and say "Hi, I'm _____, please call me this from now on, I prefer it." And they did, to her surprise. If you are being called by a name you hate, please think of the energy of that, and change it immediately. Both of these ladies are now happy with their names and it shows in their everyday smile. Just because you were either given a name or grew up being called a certain name, doesn't mean you have to keep it! Change your name, change your energy!

March 10, 2013

This is one of the worst weeks at AHIH. Everyone canceled coming to classes and then a snow storm hit and made the entire week a loss. I was at my lowest point and surrendered it all to God. Of course, I happen to be reading the <u>Moses Code</u> by James F. Twyman this week as well. The book describes giving your fear to God and let him take the final step for you. Then, when it works out in your favor, you understand you are one with God. And you have been called to act as God in the (your) world. The current world and everything in it now fades and dissolves into the Holy purpose, for it is your purpose as well. Sometimes the ego takes over, and says it can't do something, and stops trying without releasing it to God. It's the last step needed to move forward and where people stop. I'm incredibly blessed to have been able to release to God as quick as I did. I really don't care what happens now, and pray I learned the lesson!

One of the days the following week I stood in the middle of the Reiki room and prayed that the customers I needed to make the rent this month would flow in if that was God's will. By the weekend, I had one customer who spent $600 purchasing merchandise!

Reflection: Although I was in awe that it worked, I still didn't feel one with God. I didn't learn it yet, but it's coming soon! Sometimes you need to read the lesson you need to learn and let it percolate within you. I have noticed that I have learned the lesson when it is accompanied by a major emotional release….I didn't get that yet!

The Pi stone used for the Munay-Ki rites will disappear if you are done with the energy of that stone. Or, as in my case, break as it hits the bathroom floor! I fell asleep with it on my chest as I went to bed, and walked to the bathroom, in the middle of the night, clueless that it was still there. As it crashed onto the floor, I felt horrible! I just starred at it on the floor. Then I realized it fell in four equal parts in the north, south, east and west directions. HHHHMMMMM, this meant something to me. I took a picture of it, and then the next day I brought it outside. As a stone from Mother Earth, it is natural to return her there. I went to the borders of my property, and buried them in the ground in the respective directions she broke in. As I buried each one, I thanked them for their lessons, said how sorry I was that I broke them, and asked them for protection of their direction. I asked them to protect any occupants of the house, the house itself and our property. Nightly, before bed, I pray to the Laika, ask them to expand their bands of power of protection over the house to keep us safe from any negative energies or lower vibrations while we sleep. I start in the East and ask the bands of power to expand and connect with the bands of power in the west. Then I ask the West to expand and connect with the East. I then go to the South and do the same to the North. Once they are all expanded and connected with each other, I then ask them to provide a layer of protection 360 degrees around the house and property. I feel secure falling asleep!

Reflection: You can use black tourmaline or clear quartz to set up grids of protection too! The important part is to invoke their energy before going to bed. If you are connected to these stones when you place them in the earth, they will respond to you.

March 15, 2013

I gave a client a Reiki session that was intense! My hands on her neck were really hot and she said her third eye was vortexing. I was only able to work on her an hour and knew I needed to do it again. I pulled out a lot of negative electric energy from under her cheek bones. She could feel Dr. Usui and Mrs. Takata in the room helping her and of course we called in all the archangels, saints and ascended masters to help today during round two. When it was over, she asked to be given a sign and she heard that she should be working with those passing. We had talked about this before and for some reason the pieces all came together today. We both cried as this was her "AH-HA" moment. She is an amazing person who can not only help the person passing do it effortlessly, but also help the families understand the entire process. She had a very close friend recently pass who said she would help her write a book about it! We were both amazed, and grateful for the information. Such a blessing!

Reflection: I am amazed at how many people have life affirmations during Reiki sessions or attunements! On several occasions while giving attunements, I will feel intense third eye pain and can warn the Practitioner that headaches will be coming. This is really important to share as they would be taking medicines to get rid of the pain when they should be using Reiki on it.

Reflection: This world needs more people who can assist souls to heaven. It is extremely difficult as a family member to watch your loved one passing. It is harder if you know they need to be able to forgive themselves and anyone else they've had issues with in the past. Having an experienced person to discuss difficult topics with the person who is passing is what is needed. Whether this person is a clergy member, hospice worker or a person specializing in this area, they are truly angels on Earth.

March 18, 2013

I got a reading that I am like a jelly fish, I need to learn to go with the flow, shine my light in the darkness at the last minute. That is so interesting to me, as I feel that way about people in general with Reiki. Some clients try everything else first, at the last minute, when everything else has failed them, they try Reiki. They then know something has changed, and although it's good, sometimes it's too late to truly help the way it could have if only they had tried it sooner!

March 26, 2013

I look back 14 days ago and realize this must be why this is happening now. I took a Lightarian purification ring class that helps you to see the big picture! The Seraph Y angels have been working with me to see people differently. There are people in my life that I just need to release. I keep hoping that they will say "sorry" and we can move on, but it's not happening. I am starting to see the big picture now, I don't need to be liked by everyone, and I'll be ok. Human relationships are difficult because everyone has different experiences in life. Those experiences make your beliefs different from mine. The tricky part is coming together by the golden rule and keeping your mind open. Reiki has allowed my calm inner self to be able to listen with an open heart. As long as you are not hurting anyone, what difference does it make if I believe in Christ and you don't? This is what America is based on: FREEDOM! This is why people around the world want to come here! Everyone can practice what they believe, in peace. America believes in separate religions, living together peacefully. Separate, together. You feel the love in your heart for everyone. ALL YOU NEED IS LOVE!

March 27, 2013

Drum circle tonight was amazing with Sierra North. She saw me with a hammer smashing glass. She said when I was done; I lay down and cried, just surrendered to it all. Then I got up and left it all behind, I got rid of old beliefs that I was brought up with. The journey we did with her was to the Easter moon, where we asked to release stuff and asked for new stuff to replace it. Jesus showed up and I asked him if he saw the polar bear. (Why wouldn't I just be happy that Jesus was there?) He said "no." I gave in and had a conversation with Jesus instead. I asked him for financial help and was told not to worry. I asked to release negativity and worry. Sierra suggested we infuse our wishes for this year in an Easter egg and bury it in the ground. The burying of the egg represents renewal, fertility for all, with this new moon along with resurrection for Easter. I think I also asked for more clients to heal like Jesus did, I don't remember any no's from him, so I am hopeful. That was so cool to be able to converse with Jesus! He doesn't appear a lot, but it made sense that I would especially be able to communicate during Easter.

April 1, 2013

I keep thinking "keep on swimming, swimming, swimming" the song from Nemo. People have said that it takes years to become successful in a business. My issue is I just want to heal people. I don't even really care about the amount of money I put in. I want to quit my full time job. I am beginning to realize the whole business side of this is draining too much of my energy. I just keep giving it to God to handle. I realize this business was just dropped into my lap, so if it's meant to be, it will be.

Reflection: Notice the words I used here…this is draining too much of my energy. This was a big red flag that I missed.

April 17, 2013

Drum circle with Sierra North…my turn was different this time. The ladies were drumming around me and it didn't sound right to me. They typically drum together in a rhythm, but they were at all different rates, some fast, some slow. Sierra rang bells over my head and I felt my crown chakra open up. Next, my back was hot, on fire, and I was sweating! Now I was crying, not knowing what was happening, and it took me back to my first Reiki attunement experience. I wanted to know what was going on! I wasn't able to meditate, and when it was over I apologized since I had no idea why I was crying. Sierra said, "I do" and told me the story: I was in Polynesia; women were performing a ritual by a waterfall on me. I was told to drink coconut milk, that it is milk from Mother Earth and heals more than I would understand. Tons of bats then flew over my head and one landed in my hands which were tingly the whole time. I had to eat the bat for transformation, and I did. Sierra said this would lead to me having a new way to know energy. I just know- don't need to see, feel or hear it. I'll just know. What was interesting to me is that yesterday we did a Lightarian class where we were told there will be things we will just know….so fascinating to me!

Reflection: I believe I do just know some things automatically. People will try to convince me otherwise, but somehow I know the truth. Maybe this is Archangel Gabriel working even more closely with me!

April 20, 2013

Upon leaving AHIH tonight, I looked at the sky and saw the moon surrounded by clouds. The clouds were in a star shape around the moon, I wish I had a cool phone to take a picture! This image will live in my mind forever!

April 23, 2013

I smelled Granma's tuna today. It is a distinct smell, and I have not thought about that smell in a long time. As a matter of fact, since I don't smell much, and no one else could smell it, I think it was just her way of getting me to notice that she is around. I should ask for my ancestors help more often. She had given me the silver Mother Mary medal necklace, and I wear it daily now and think of her often. It was so interesting that I could SMELL the tuna as well.

My lease is up on July 31, 2013 and due to issues with my landlord, I can't remain here. (Is this what I was feeling April 1?) I hope that my time is not up yet I still believe everything happens for a reason. I think about getting a partner to come into AHIH and put in some money to keep this going. I have ideas to make this an even better place. This is not something I am supposed to do on my own, and I am ready to take this to the next level! I have seen AHIH heal so many people, I am ready to make it bigger! As I realize in years to come, a piece of land in a commercial area with these specifications is NOT cheap. I am willing to wait it out, and I think back on the drum circle where I was smashing glass, and leaving it all behind.

May 6, 2013

We do a class to help us set our intentions with Sierra North. As we did a journey to the West, I heard a deep voice man talking while Sierra was drumming. I've never heard anyone before, I jumped and opened my eyes, there was no one else here, just our female clientele. Everyone heard him, but no one understood the message. UGH! Why don't they just say it so we can understand? I want my ear chakras to open more!

May 15, 2013

Drum circle with Sierra North was beyond anything I could ever have imagined. We drummed around Sierra last, as a thank you for her class. I typed the following to her in an email because it was beyond anything I would have been able to talk about....part of me thought she'd think I was crazy!

While drumming with everyone else, I got the feeling I was supposed to use Sierra's drum because this was a special ceremony, and yet we had already started and I didn't want to interrupt your journey to ask if I could use your drum.

Nothing major came to me while drumming with everyone except this was very special. I kept asking why and finally got the answer: to prepare you for the next part of your life. Then my heart just rushed with love and I could feel a soul connection with you, we are soul sisters. I started at the twelfth chakra and brought down this incredible light. I kept moving it down your chakras to the earth star chakra. This all happened while I was drumming in the back of you.

That's about when everyone stopped drumming. Now I thought, I should stop, since they did, and then I heard the drum or guides say "not yet". So I continued, and I thought this is dumb. No one drums alone. Then I was told again this is a special ceremony. Then I thought, well, it's my place, I guess I can drum by myself. I asked what the ceremony was for tonight. It was a blessing, at first for me to thank you for everything you've done for all the customers in the store. I started crying thinking this was the end of our work together. Then, God, Jesus, Buddha came to Bless you. I had to drum around you three times, once for each. Jesus forgave your sins, and I felt him kiss your feet as I drummed more blessings into your hands for healing. This was so sacred, I kept crying and the drum kept drumming, I swear I was NOT in control of the drumming. I kept thinking, I need to stop, everyone is watching me cry and drum....but I couldn't. So, I kept drumming until they were done. I honestly felt like the drum had this agenda, and I was just there to help her. It was as if I was watching my hand hit the drum, and I should have been tired, as it was a fast beat and had a certain rhythm to it. But when it was over, it was as if I had been doing it all my life. Not tired at all, and actually felt like we had accomplished something amazing together!

I was listening to everyone else in the class tell you about seeing you in a white dress and that you had white light in your neck. I didn't "see" that, but felt it. It was like you were Mother Mary of our time. I was so EXTREMELY grateful and blessed to be in your presence. I don't think I have much time left with you, but I know that I was there at a pivotal point in your life. These are the things we remember. A night I will not ever forget.

Sierra responded: Tears of truth flooded to my eyes and what you saw and felt was what I saw too. I am grateful to you as I fully understand how much you and your shop have allowed and encouraged me to grow and remember. I love being a part of AHIH and I promise to you I will remain with you as long as I am able. I think it's longer than you think too! I still have much learning, growing, and remembering to do and you and the wonderful people who come there push me along on my journey. My love to you and may all the blessings I receive shower over you as well! I meant to tell you not to pack that drum. It is yours. Your hearts have merged. That drum is my gift to you and I am honored to give it.

I responded: I am so glad that we had the same visions, as I always worry what I am going to say is not what is really happened for you....then again, maybe it doesn't matter. It is so interesting that they were the same! I was blessed to be able to be there to do this, and it was an eye opener for me in many ways. I believe if the right people are in the room together, the energy will bring what needs to happen. THANK YOU is not enough to convey the gratitude I have for the drum. I needed to have that very experience with you to really understand that it was mine. If it had not been as powerful, I would not have said it's mine. I still have no real idea what I "need" the drum for as I am a novice at this and don't know if I'll ever have a similar experience. It seems like a luxury to have, and something to only use for special occasions. I hope that makes sense to you. Many thanks for all you do for us!

Reflection: Sierra goes to Nepal and takes on the name Radhe that means Mary. She does a lot of healing work with Mother Mary. I feel honored that she took the name I know was meant for her!

May 2, 2013

Sierra's house to paint my drum! I am so extremely nervous and so many things are going through my head. What if I mess up the drum? I don't think I should do this, maybe it's best to let Sierra paint it for me! She says I can do it, and I keep saying I can't draw….how is this going to come out? I smudge the drum before working on each step. There is a drum ceremony first, to find out what the drum is supposed to be painted. I worried that it would be something I would not be able to paint, of course that is silly. Each drum finds the right drummer for the specific purpose they need. Mine tells me she is a healing drum and needs to be white in the middle. The chakra colors coming towards the middle with red on the outside coming to the white in the middle. She needs to be sparkly, bright colors and leave the middle open for something to be determined. I asked if she was male or female and got BOTH as the answer, but I still prefer to call her female. Day One: I painted the middle white and kept swirling the paint, almost in a trance mode and finally saw a rose coming in the center. I used yellow with it at first, but the color wasn't right, then added gold….because the chakra colors should turn to gold, of course! Next the chakra colors went all the way around it, gradually getting bigger. The red is the last color on the outside and looks like spinning chakras, or feathers moving. Number 7 keeps coming up, inner life, wisdom, 7 Heavens, birth and rebirth, religious strength, sacred vows, spiritual ritual, solitude, analysis, contemplation, intuition, dreams, visions, philosophical and metaphysical studies. The natural stones I brought originally to make a curtain decoration have now become what I am using on the sides of the drum for decoration. Who would have thought that's what I needed them for, many months ago, when I bought them?

The journey to the drum to find out her name, 7 Heavens! Her job is to teach everyone about the chakras, colors and balance for all of them. I need to instruct, have all colors of stones and candles on hand at all times for balance at the store. I will use this drum for people with issues as they come into purchase items. She will be in the new store with all new colors and ideas….more to come. I need to journey with her weekly if not more when I am upset, she will lead me the right way. Once everyone is in balance with colors, they will understand the chakras and be able to help each other more. I need ribbons on the beater as well as the outside of the drum.

Initiation to the Drum, you beat to your own heartbeat and then connect to Mother Earth. Next, you connect the drum to you. Once it's connected to you, it's like a major chakra attunement. My entire body was hot! Next the drum beat gets faster and that's how you know you are attuned to it. Next you take the beater and put the drum beat into each chakra. When this is done, the beat returns to the original slow beat. Next, we drummed for each other. I learned that the colors resonate with a different sound. I drummed for Sierra and noticed when I got to her root and beat the drum on the red part, it sounded tinny. I beat the drum all around the chakra color until she finally sounded "right". I can tell this is going to be a lot of work, but a powerful healing drum. It took an entire weekend to paint, and repaint….the journey is listening to your intuition, and trusting the info coming in is exactly what is needed. A lot of patience is needed, and for me, that was an instrumental part of my learning this weekend! I am looking forward to finding out more about what I can accomplish with her, and I can't wait until the next drum circle!

Reflection: I never would have believed I would be the owner of a drum. She has become a "go to" for clearing chakras. If the person is sitting in a chair it is easy to drum around the person and hear where the chakra is muddied vs. clear. I continually drum in that area until the sound changes. I am able to now drum and journey at the same time, which was difficult to learn at first. Once the drum understands what it is you need she helps you by almost drumming by herself so that I can focus on getting answers to issues at hand. I am grateful to have this most amazing tool to help heal with Reiki.

June 5, 2013

I buy a Gold Sheen Black Obsidian, and have never been so excited by a rock! I ask it a question and it answers in the form of a picture in the stone. I asked if someone was telling me the truth and I saw a top hat in the stone…it made no sense to me, then I looked a little more to the left and saw a rabbit….and put the two together to get magician, what you see is not real….wow!

Reflection: Over the years I use this stone when I seem stuck for an answer, it has never been wrong. I do not let anyone else touch the stone, as I only want it to vibrate to my energy. I think this is the only stone that I don't let anyone else hold. This is not a stone that is easy to find, and I am grateful to have a wand of it!

June 12, 2013

I have a power animal retrieval session with Sierra North. She starts with a drum ceremony to connect with her guides to find your power animal. She gets the information needed then blows the energy of the animal into your crown chakra and heart. I was seated and tried to meditate while she was drumming to see if I could figure out the correct animal as well. I thought I had it, a fox. I didn't know anything about a fox, but I would learn. These conversations were going on in my head. Then my thoughts stopped as I heard the drum get louder. Sierra didn't take long before putting this energy into my crown. It was intensely hot! Then she put it in my heart, which was also hot. As she proceeded to sit down she was as red as could be and said, "Oh my God that was intense, and amazing!" As she looked at me I had tears in my eyes as she said "holy crap, that was intense" She sat down and had some water. I finally said" what's my power animal?" she said "you are a dragon." Now, I know nothing about the dragon and thought it was odd since dragon is a mythical animal, not real to me. So I said, "no, that's not it, isn't it a fox"? She laughed, and said "dragon". She told me Shaman's all want to find out their dragon and it's not something she'd ever just pull up for someone, Dragon must appear for you. Sierra's journey took her to her power animal to find mine, and then ALL her power animals showed up and she got worried since that doesn't happen, ever. Then she was taken to the sea, and out comes my iridescent blue majestic dragon. She said it is as big as the mountains and was the sea dragon but also represented all elements. He came out of the sea, to the sky, and then dived back into the ocean. He came back to Sierra with a lapis ocean color pearl, vast and immense. The pearl is the energy of the dragon, particular to that dragon, representing pure light. Dragons are guardians of the portal/gateways. If you look into the eye of the dragon it is the death of ego. Dragon medicine is transformation and manifestation. Be careful for what you ask for, and remember to ask for the highest and greatest good. I was shocked! Honestly, I know nothing about dragons. The skeptic in me said, well that's weird. After hearing all the other people tell me about their real animal guides, I don't know what to do with this information. A few days later, I found a picture of what he looks like and send it to Sierra for verification. At least I now have an idea of what he looks like, and now I need to find out his name.

Reflection: I found out the dragon's name is Zaque. To date Zaque shows up when I am giving Reiki to clear blockages or when the person needs an extra energy boost. I don't specifically call him to help, but I know when he is here as I begin to rock back and forth and my hands move in the same motion. I purchased a statue that resembles him and keep it on my Reiki altar along with pictures of Dr. Usui and Mrs. Takata, as he is a most valuable guide in healing.

June 25, 2013

A client who I have been giving Reiki to weekly tells me "I don't feel supported by God." My stomach instantly got upset and I had a tough time digesting the words. I finally asked "why?" She felt as if she was on her life path, which was perfect, and then something happened and took her into despair, disappointment and uncertainty. I said "maybe you needed to experience those things to bring you to the path you are on now. She said "I feel stuck, not sure where this is." She is now angry with me because in her mind this is not the path she is supposed to be on. Part of her wants to go back to another point in her past and start again from there. I cried as I drove home that night, knowing I didn't get through to her. She heard me, but I could tell by the look in her eyes, she didn't understand it in her soul. There is a lot of anger here that I need to help her work through; this is going to take time for her to get back to love.

Reflection: I think about her situation and how that could depress you. Depression is not something a person chooses to be in, nor can snap out of it. Depression involves several stages: shock/denial, anger, sadness and finally acceptance. In the months to come, we explore all of these over and over again, finding a deeper level of healing with each session. Reiki along with a licensed therapists help was exactly what brought her to an understanding of her new path in life.

We need to deal with the deeper meaning of our illness. Ask yourself "What does this illness mean to me? What can I learn from it?" Illness can be seen as a message from your body that says: "Wait a minute, something is wrong. What is it?" Your return to health requires more than taking a prescription. Personal change is required to lead you back to the source that caused the disease in the first place. By listening to this guidance, you will be back into health, and more connected to the Divinity within.

We have the Seraphim V class to release the cloak of fear. I was so nervous about it that I didn't even do the first class, but took the second offering of it. On June 29, I have Crystal Vibrations Jewelry owners Stacy Goforth and Valinda Salva in the store. Valinda hears me talking about the internet not working, the electric switch at the house sparking and a light not on at AHIH. Valinda says to me, it has to do with my personal power. She offers to do a quick conscious access healing session and gives me the orange fearlessness bracelet to hold. I put it on and start crying. She says I have an implant in the back of my head where the V is that hurt after releasing the fear with Seraphim V. She takes it out and I end up purchasing the fearlessness bracelet, the second one I own. I bought the awakening and transforming one when I first got to the store, and it helped calm my nerves, and helped with menopausal issues too! I told them they need to add menopausal support to the things it can help with, as it sure helped me!

Reflection: I own many of these bracelets and wear them as necklaces and anklets too! I am so confident in the ability of them to assist in healing that I sell them at A Hand in Healing!

July 11, 2013

Two new Reiki 1 Practitioners – one was in a religious position for work and was looking for a way to connect all the things he's learned. I called him before class to see if he had any questions and instinctively knew I needed to call when I did. He said in class that the phone call came while he was driving and he was questioning if he should take the class. He said it was because of the call that he did! I notice I get urgent "do it now" messages. When I think I can just tell myself I can do it later, it continues to bother me until I do it. Learning to trust that intuition is critical, and it is a part of the third eye opening even more.

July 12, 2013

The dragon workshop with Sierra North. Since the power animal retrieval, I wanted to do this class! The journey we took was different than any other I've had, because I decided I wanted to lay on the floor. As the journey started it was clear quickly that I needed to sit up, Indian style instead. Upon sitting I called to Zaque in my head and asked him to show me one piece of info. Somehow I asked for healing of the third eye, which includes the ears, nose, eyes, and teeth. My body started moving back and forth, in a rocking motion and my hands were getting energy. I don't know how long it was, but it was interesting and worrisome to me. Sierra verified I was receiving a healing. The rocking is when energy gets stuck and is shifting…she has had it happen several times.

Reflection: I notice each time Zaque comes to help me with a healing the rocking occurs. I don't ask for him, he just appears and I begin moving back and forth. I know that he is needed for deeper healings. He comes a lot during Reiki attunements, and I am always grateful!

July 17, 2013

Ignite Your Spirit Healing. Maitreya is from Australia and is with ShantiMission.org. He did an Ignite Your Spirit healing on me. He asked which chakras needed help, I said 3rd eye and wealth. He sang with a guitar in points and asked me questions: "What is the big picture of the new vision of AHIH," I cried as I was not sure. He said I was a World Class Reiki Master and teacher, which took me off guard, as I don't think of myself in that way. I released all past thoughts about money, and that it would flow gracefully to me now. I prayed he was right!

Reflection: Looking back at this, I can see that although the mind wanted the money to flow, I knew that was not for my highest and greatest good at this location. Having these healings are only as good as what work YOU are willing to do with them. I certainly was NOT there yet. My mind was focused on too many other things for my Reiki work to be at the forefront. This was not why I opened this store and it hasn't hit me yet that I need to take a step back and figure this out.

July 31, 2013

Closing A Hand in Healing in Farmington. I knew drum circle would be amazing the last evening in this location! My third eye headache was back and someone offered to Reiki it for me, and I saw colors, purple, green, yellow, and white light. Sierra North came in to set up a Despachio and it was perfect as I had Reiki hands over my eyes. I cried while putting in my blessings for the Despachio. I was so grateful for the time I had here, and happy with all that I learned. I gave Reiki to everyone – one person called it "blow your face off Reiki" as her third eye opened. Zaque helped to blow the energy through her faster. One said she's never experienced such intense Reiki, I said "thanks to Zaque!" We ended with both me and Sierra in the center and everyone drummed around us. It was a lot of energy, so much that I was giving it back to those drumming. I've never heard it so loud. It brought up a new idea of doing drum circle for pair's: mother and daughter, husband and wife....imagine the power! Everyone helped pack up, and I said thank you to each room, called back my power and left with tears of joy. I wasn't skeptical anymore!

Reflection: While working here I also worked a 30 hour p/week paid job. Every day I prayed to get the energy I needed, and I did. There were days I didn't understand how I was able to keep going. This tells me that the work is needed and somehow I would find a way to continue.

August 30, 2013

This past week I had the worst menstrual cycle ever....sweating, diarrhea, feeling faint. I knew something was different as the week went on and I kept getting weaker. They symptoms changed, I was also now out of breathe, had heart palpitations and tingling in my left food up to the knee. I googled my symptoms and found they are all symptoms of B 12 anemia. The very same thing my mother had been diagnosed with a while ago. I got a blood test on Thursday am, and by Thursday night the Doctor called and said I had extreme anemia. The Dr. said, "I don't want to scare you, but you need a blood transfusion." I got off the phone and cried. BLOOD TRANSFUSION? He said if anything changed overnight to call him immediately on his cell phone. Oh My God, I thought I was going to die that night. I have never had any other ailments and I was so scared. Sleeping was next to impossible so I prayed a lot. Prayer is so different when there is a potential life and death element involved. I prayed harder, longer and more intensely than I have in a long time. The next morning we called and the Dr. said to go to the emergency room for outpatient treatment. We were there at 9am, figured I'd be home in a few hours. The ER Dr. said "we need to figure out why you are anemic." I said, "My mother and father were both anemic." I was thinking isn't that enough? But, the testing began…Chest xray, EKG, ultra sounds, blood test and more blood tests….I am thinking, "hey people, you realize I am here to get some blood right?" I felt like every drop they took away from me was making me weaker and weaker. A few times while waiting I thought I would faint. I didn't want to faint as I felt they would do something even more drastic. Although I was praying to God to help me, I was also at the point where I was so weak and light headed I thought I would float above my body. In this state I know I promised God to help heal more people with Reiki if I lived. If he needed me to go, I understood as well. For the first time, I was not afraid to die. I accepted that I was not in control here and was ok with it. I thought about my children and husband who is sitting here holding my hand and knew they would be fine. Maybe that was all I needed to do in life, maybe bringing two wonderful children into the world with my husband was my soul purpose. None of the other things in my life mattered now. I put all my heart and soul into Gods hands. I surrendered to God. I had heard others use the terminology before, but never understood it until now. All my life I felt I was in control, as a team with God. Suddenly, I knew I never really was in control. Now I was finally ready for God to take the wheel and I would just go along for the ride. I surrendered, and I finally understood! As soon as I said it in my head and with compassion in my heart, there was the answer. I am one with God. This is the meaning of I AM! I never felt this peaceful in my life! This new sense of being filled my eyes with tears and put a smile on my lips. Reading this even now brings back the tears in my eyes. This was a life changing moment, one I will NEVER forget.

At 1pm they finally start the blood transfusion, and it took 4 hours but my blood count had not increased enough to be released. I had to be admitted and have another transfusion. Since I surrendered to God, I felt blessed or holy....I can't describe the feeling of absolute bliss inside me. I was grateful for everything. When I think about it, that incredible thankful feeling still washes over me. When the nurse arrived with the next bag of blood at 10pm, I asked if I could pray over it first. She agreed and I cried, so grateful to whoever had donated these bags of blood for me to live. I asked God to bless them. I thought about the fact that I would never know these angels. It bothered me that I could never even write them a letter to say thank you. I asked Reiki to fill the blood with whatever I needed to be healthy, whole, well and complete. I asked God to remove any toxins from the blood so that I could go home. By 3:15 am I was told the blood level was high enough that I could go home in the am if it remained where it was, oh I was the happiest I have been since my last child was born! In the days to follow, I realize that blood equates to the joy in life. I did receive joy. I had been too busy trying to make everyone else happy, that I was not enjoying my time, not reflecting on the glory of it all. Having anemia slows you down physically, so it gave me plenty of thinking time. I realize that although I want to bring everyone with me on this journey, and let them experience the light as I have, not everyone will come along. I pray even harder, more intensely, and longer than I ever have in the past. I ask for Divine guidance for everyone that I meet. I hope that I may bring them what they need to advance on their path as well. I feel like I have a lot of work to do and know this is why I am impatient. I am so afraid that I may die before I help more people, the urgency made me feel nervous. I want the people in my life to understand and support me enough to understand why Reiki and A Hand in Healing are so important to so many customers. I hope and pray it is a long life journey!

Reflection: I needed this time to be able to take a step back and evaluate what is happening in my life. I had to close A Hand in Healing and move it back to my house. I spent months looking for the perfect new location, never to find it. I hated that at first, because I didn't want it at my house. But, of course, this was needed. This home retreat made me realize who would still support me and my dream. That one thing helped me reshape my dream. Sometimes you are so busy doing, that you don't have time to figure out what is working and what isn't working. The anemia let me find my joy in a way I didn't even know existed. If there is a point in your life that feels like a disappointment, try to settle into it. It takes at least a month to go through all the emotions. Then once you are calm enough, the understanding starts to come to light.

November 14, 2013

Reiki 2 class (part one) with a future Reiki Master

This Practitioner's attunement was the calmest I have ever felt. The whole room was like Christmas Eve, calm and peaceful. She said it was very physical for her, healing her. The second attunement was angelic, she had this little smile on her face the whole time; she said it was like she graduated and everyone she knew was bringing her gifts! She said she felt complete.

November 20, 2013

First drum circle with Sierra North since she returned from Nepal!

Sierra had told me months ago that she may not be going to Nepal due to finances. I had no idea how to fix this issue but told her she was going. I had no idea where that thought even came from; I had no real plans to get her there. Something just made me say it and now I was on the hook to produce it. We did fundraisers, and set up a GOFUNDME page explaining her journey and got her there! I asked her to bring me back a rock from the mountain Achhapuchhre in the Aunapurna Himalayan range she climbed. It actually had the shape of the mountain as well! Sierra brought rough rose quartz with her, washed it in a sacred river and gave us all a piece of it. It has a lot of energy, and mine actually looks like the mountain she climbed! She also gifted me with an aquamarine necklace, which seems to have every metaphysical property I need, of course. I meditated with it and another guardian angel is Emanuel. I didn't find out until Dec 22 that he is Jesus. PERFECT!

We had ten people for drum circle tonight, and it was finished an hour earlier than normal. I was wondering if it was the new rocks that helped us get through energy blocks quicker. Also this week my Reiki classes went faster....which was odd because they all had major issues. One was going for a gall bladder issue tomorrow, another with stomach issues and the third with major issues from the past. They were all amazed at the amount of energy they removed with the selenite stick. It actually feels heavy too, when removing old negative energy. I hold it on the negative energy and ask it to please remove any negative energy that doesn't belong to _____. In the name of God, you must go into this Selenite stick. God has more energy and light than _____ will ever have and loves you. In the name of God, leave _____ now. You will feel the cord attached to the person as you move or pull this stick up vertically into the air. It's heavy, it's thick, but keeping pulling up until your arm can't go up any further. Then ask Archangel Michael to cut it with his blue light sword. As soon as it is done, I put the selenite back in the spot and do it again until I know that the energy there has changed. You can feel a difference once it is cleared. Then ask Archangel Raphael to come and fill the spot with unconditional loving healthy, whole, complete healing cells. Always thank them when you are done.

Reflection: Selenite is my all-time go to rock....I sleep with it too! Before bed I use it to sweep over every chakra and ask it to remove any negative energy I picked up from any people, place or things I have been in contact with during the day. I leave it in my pillow case and by the time morning comes, I feel totally refreshed and ready to go! If you don't already have one, this should be first on your list of stones to have available for Reiki treatments. It is especially good for working on anyone with back issues, simply put it on the side of the spine and Reiki over it.

January 14, 2014

A client asked me my opinion on buying horses. In the middle of the night I wake up with the answer that there are two white horses she needs to see in another state. I ask my guide three times if this is correct info, and I finally send her a text to let her know....still feeling silly. She responds that she is going to see them the next day, and that she is in that state... WOW! That really was amazing for me – my intuition is finally opening up!

January 26, 2014

I am preparing pork chops in a plastic bag with bread crumbs. I used a bread and butter knife to stab the pork chop to get it out of the bag. The second time I was not paying attention and stabbed the knife through my ring finger at the webbing between the fingers. I held it up and noticed I could see ligaments and said out loud "Reiki now, Reiki now, Reiki now" and then told my husband we were going to the emergency room. At the time, I could not focus on doing any Reiki on myself but I knew I needed it immediately. This is absolutely the right method to use to start Reiki if you are in a state of shock and can't find the clarity any other way. I could feel my hand start to tingle and I knew my guides were with me. Some derma bond and a tetanus shot and I was fine!

Reflection: In emergencies, saying "Reiki now" absolutely works to get your guides to help you! Say thank you later if you are mentally unable to at the moment.

February 21, 2014 Drum Circle with Sierra North

We journeyed to the Heart Chakra and the Egyptian Goddess Ma'at. Ma'at weighs your heart in comparison to an ostrich feather. The idea is that your heart should be lighter than the feather. As Sierra drums, you go into a meditation to talk to Ma'at. I instantly saw her and asked if she would weigh my heart, so I hand it to her and of course it is heavier. I asked how to make it lighter, and she said I need to stop comparing my life to others. No one is the same; we all have different experiences which makes us grow at different rates. I also need to do more fun things, sing and dance. Relax more. I asked if she would take out anything I don't need or "dismember the heart" and asked her to heal the anemia. She pulled out what looked like a tube and said the anemia was healed. I asked that it now make the correct amount of hems so that the blood is good. Then she gave it back, and I returned to the room. When it was my turn for being in the middle of the drum circle, I sat in the green heart chakra chair with my feet on the peach selenite slab. I found myself thinking about how grateful I am for my heart. That it is THE organ that keeps you alive. Obviously, I knew this before, but I was feeling so blessed inside. I started to cry as I was trusting with all my heart in the people working on me. I was then told by Ma'at that I need to see myself as GOD, only ask for help, that all grief of all past issues was now healed. I need to see myself in all others with compassion. LOVE IS ALL WE NEED.

When it was over, I could not stand. My legs were weak, and I had to sit back down. Sierra told me she saw my parents and ancestors in back of me, and my sons and future family in front of me. I was the light that connects them all. She then cut them all away so my light could shine brighter and be even better for all. Wow, I was scared. As a Mom, I always put family first. But I am at that point where the boys are grown and I should be putting me first now. What a night, a lot of growing still happening!

Reflection: Selenite slabs are incredible to own. My dream is to own more so that I have my feet on one, am sitting on one and can hold them in each hand as well. I am not surprised that this is the only time I decided to use this during a meditation with Sierra. Selenite can be used with past life work and healing of it, and gives you an understanding of your place in the world. It is easier to do mediations with it, and I think I got just what was needed this night!

March 22, 2014

This is the beginning of something I never would have imagined happening to me. I woke with a very heavy heart chakra. I tried to figure out what it was, or who it was from, and it eluded me. I went on Facebook and found that a cousin had passed of a massive heart attack. I just broke down crying. The weird part was that I didn't know him in person. My son just recently connected with him by email and they were starting small conversations. I knew I had to reach out to his soul. I found out that he didn't want to leave his son who is in a coma in a nursing home. I said to him, you need to go to heaven with Jesus as you can do more for him there than here, for him and all of us. I said this over and over, as he wanted to stay here, and my heart knew he needed to leave. I finally found myself saying, you need to trust me on this, go with Jesus. I asked for my heart to have no pain when he is there. Most of it finally went away but wonder if the pain I am feeling now is from his son?

Reflection: This was a month after the heart chakra journey. I know that journey was pivotal in changing my overall understanding of love and the heart. I believe this was needed to bring me to the next level of heart work I will do from a distance.

August 4, 2014

I feel like I've shifted into the 5th dimension! I feel lighter, taller, straighter, kinder, more patient even! Sierra says that the Lion's gate portal started 8/8-8/25 to shift us into the 5th dimension. The earth and all humans are shifting into a new consciousness of love, compassion and peace. I feel it today!

August 23, 2014

I went to one of my Reiki Master Practitioners house to see her space. She will be opening her home for business soon, and offered to give me Reiki there. I get on the table, she puts her hands on my head and for the first time ever, I felt Reiki leaving my head to go into her hands. I waited for a few minutes to pay attention to what was happening. I was not giving her Reiki on purpose, yet it was definitely energy leaving my head. She said "it feels like you are giving Reiki to me." I said, "I know, I feel it to, but I don't know why." We sat there a few more moments and I finally got the message that I was supposed to give Reiki to her. She said, "No, that's not what we are supposed to be doing." Finally, I insisted, "let's trade places." The reason was so I could evaluate her space. As I gave her Reiki I was able to see the energy of the room and make suggestions to be sure the energy stayed in her room, not leave through windows. Now, any time a Reiki Practitioner wants to start a business, I ask to go and evaluate their space. The Feng Shui of a space is very important to the sacred feeling you get when receiving Reiki. Your head and/or feet should not be in front of a window, where you feel all your energy leaving. We moved some screens to block a window, used black tourmaline in front of the TV to absorb negative energy and added grounding items under the Reiki table. Perfect, now it felt better!

October 17, 2014

A client told me 15 months ago she came down with bronchitis, and it has taken on a form of spots in her lungs that doctors are watching. CAT scans are showing they are getting bigger and it could turn into a lung disease. I asked her if there was anything going on at that time 15 months ago. Did she have a car accident or major life change? She said "Oh my goodness, yes! I was on vacation with my children and was emotionally devastated. I wondered where I fit in, I felt rejected, no longer needed."

I told her about The Roby Chart by Cheryl Roby and how it shows you physically where the emotions become disease. Then I told her that lungs are the ability to take in life. She said "Oh my goodness, my life is my love of my children now. I've been through divorce and wonder if I can ever find love again. I told her we will work on removing negative beliefs. I told her she can have enough love for her children and find a new life partner. She just needed to hear those words, as it gave her a whole new outlook. During the Reiki session she released a lot of emotion, especially from the heart chakra, where I gave her Reiki for at least half an hour. When we were done, she felt lighter, and looked radiant, so I am hopeful something changed. She took Reiki 1 class as well.

November 8, 2014

Today I have a Reiki treatment for a client with a thyroid issue. I wore all blue this day to deal with this throat chakra issue. I feel a place on the right side shoulder where a spot is bothering me. Many times I get information before the client even arrives, which helps me prepare. I look into stones needed and begin prayers for her complete healing, if that is what she will allow. During the session something popped, we both heard it and right after that she saw a white light. She asked me why I put the light on. I replied that I still had my hands on her and what she saw was God healing her!

Reflection: Many people see the white light during Reiki sessions. This is their connection with God or guardian angels.

November 18, 2014

I have a Reiki treatment with another Reiki Master who has an amazing rock collection! She placed peach aventurine on my heart chakra and I felt heaviness like someone pushing down on my chest. She gave me one to take home and I saw an angel inside a heart on the stone, which I slept with that night. My heart thumped loudly, before I was able to settle down into a great night's sleep. In the am, the angel was gone and the heart shape was not the same. My heart chakra was definitely worked on by this stone, and I was so grateful!

Reflection: When picking out stones to buy I often look to see if I can find an angel in them. Most of the time I don't see them until I get home, sometimes months later!

November 30, 2014

I woke at 2am with heart pain again, and held green kyanite at the heart chakra for hours to alleviate it. Again, I hear from a cousin that another cousin died of congestive heart failure. Now, the red flags are going off! I am getting incoming information from family with heart issues. My empathic "ears" are now on full alert. I need to tune into WHO the pain is coming from!

December 6, 2014

My cousin who was in the nursing home for over 8 years passed. I really believe his Dad passed first, nine months earlier, to be able to bring his son home.

A client was having surgery. I knew when the surgery was supposed to be over, and 45 minutes later when I had not heard any news from her family, I decided to send her Reiki. After I called in her I AM Presence I get the direct feeling she is standing beside her body in the recovery room. I asked, "What are you doing?" She said, "I am trying to decide if I want to go back." The conversation took a turn I had not expected but my subconscious mind knew immediately what to say next, there was no thought process, it just flowed. "What about your grandchildren?" "Oh yeah" she said and got right back into her body. I sent her more distance Reiki, and did a healing attunement for a smooth transition and recovery. After I finished I sent her family a text and said "she will be fine, it just took longer to come back with the anesthesia." The Dr. verified that it took longer in recovery than normal but that she was fine. A lot of times when people go through surgery, they have the opportunity to decide whether they should still be here. She was clearly on the fence, but I was able to ask just the right questions to get her to return. This was not me; I just am the conduit for God to work through me.

Reflection: I often wonder what would have happened had I NOT sent Reiki at that time. Then again, everything happens for a reason. The incredible urge to send Reiki at that time tells me it was the right thing to do. I listen with my heart, it never steers me in the wrong direction. This brings up another point about prayer. Be sure to send prayers to people having surgeries before and after the surgery.

December 18, 2014

Reiki Master Attunements for three Masters tonight! They have worked hard on their own healing and I was so proud to make them official masters tonight! I called in God, Dr. Usui, Mrs. Takata, Jesus, Mary all our spiritual guides, angels, saints, animal guides and loved ones of the light. I asked that they all get what they needed to be exceptional Reiki Masters. It was like giving birth, I was so emotional at the end. After giving them two attunements in a row, I sat down and cried. I felt the love come through my heart chakra and to each of them. It felt like a sister-soul connection. We sat in a circle and when I was done, everyone opened their eyes. I gave them each their certificate and hugged and cried with them. It was a moment I will always remember. After being with them for a year, I will miss the camaraderie of the group. They are simply amazing women whom I love.

I read this to them:

The Reiki Master title comes with great responsibility. As masters, you hold the key to healing everyone. Everything. Everywhere. When I decided to teach Reiki to others, I knew this was a part of who I am and part of my legacy. When I die I want people to remember the good I did and Reiki is my voice to get the healing message out. Reiki is a spiritual journey that heals you first, taking you down roads that you will never forget. You learn that to heal, you need to remember and come from a place of peace in your heart. This one lesson is the component you will use again and again in healing others. You have learned how to do that in class and real life. I am so proud of each of you! You reached deep to bring out the very best of you. You did the hard work and it shows in who you are today! Reiki Master doesn't stop here, with each student you teach and each Reiki session you give, it will continue to grow stronger. The learning gets deeper and you figure out new things you didn't know today. I encourage you to remain friends, share your stories and grow together to heal one and all. Thank you for blessing me with your friendship, it means more than all the money in the world. May you bless everyone you meet in your life. Congratulations, I am proud to call you Reiki Masters! Namaste!

The following day, one of the new Reiki Masters texted me: "I wish everyone on Mother Earth could feel this way." One of the others said: "What you did last night was so selfless and the ultimate act of unconditional love to all of us. 2014 was a year of transformation for me. I had ups and downs of emotions and had to go through the process. My guides told me during my attunement "she has completed her healing on you. My eyes are welling up as I'm typing this; I feel an overwhelming sense of gratitude." A third said, "I am really glad you teach Reiki the way you do, as a sacred calling and not to be taken lightly. A master has to show experience and a dedication to Reiki. From a client standpoint, you really want someone who has spent time learning their craft. Thank you!"

Reflection: My Usui Reiki Master class is not a quick process; it generally takes a year to complete. In addition to all the lessons on how to pass attunements, each individual takes part in their own personal, loving transformation. Everyone has baggage to leave behind, hearts to mend and lessons to learn. I work with them as a group and individually as everyone has different needs. In addition to the physical energy required, the chakra work, working with guides, and vibrational changes all take time. There are days when you feel light headed, dizzy and nauseated. It is all part of the transition from the old you to an awesome teacher! Building a practice takes time, but you get what you can handle, even as a Reiki Master. The right students for YOU appear because YOU can help them. Have faith that you have crossed into their path at the perfect, divine time!

January 2015

A client asks me to send Reiki to a family member who needed a heart pump, and in time, a heart transplant. I used all my heart chakra stones and the snowflake obsidian with a hole on the left side, Shiva stone, aphollite, and rose quartz. I then asked if the family member would accept distance Reiki, the answer was yes. I began Reiki and asked if the family member believed everything happens for a reason. The question instantly came up "why do I have to be sick now?" My guides are getting information from the family members guides, as I didn't think about how to answer these questions, they just came through me. "You are young." The family member says, "I don't deserve a heart, others have children, families, I don't." I said, "Because of your youth, you have a greater chance of leaving a legacy to get people to be organ donors. Your story will be known. This is your purpose." She replied with wide eyes "OOOOOHHHHH" she gave me a hug and said "I can do that!" I saw the family member now as confident because she would now get what is supposed to be in order to fulfill her purpose.

Reflection: Update, she did get the heart transplant and is getting physical therapy as of this book! I am always surprised with the reaction of clients during distance Reiki. I don't plan the conversation in my head, I just allow the guides to talk to each other. As long as it is for the client's highest and greatest good, that is all I can do. No matter how it works, it gives the client hope just to be able to ask questions. I have witnessed this over and over, giving distance Reiki to those who are at a time of great health challenges. The will overcomes the obstacles if you know your reason/purpose. I chatted with the client the day after. The client also sent distance Reiki and acknowledged that the family member understood her purpose now. This is very easy to do when the family member is not in your immediate family, but very difficult when it is. There is so much emotional attachment, it may be best to let someone outside the family member circle send distance Reiki with this type of purpose.

January 2015

A client's mom passed and she has been trying to connect with her mom. During her Reiki session, she told me she saw herself swimming in a lake. When she came out, her Mom was waiting on the beach, wearing a white spaghetti strap dress, no shoes. She took her daughters hand and smiled, she wanted to run with her daughter on the beach. The client was so overcome with emotion; she came out of the journey. She said she had never done this while awake before and was so very grateful as she now knew her mom was ok and in heaven. She said this was definitely a true vision. "That was exactly what I was waiting for, confirmation that she is ok and happy. And it goes to show that we have a Loving God. Because she isn't being punished; instead, he made her an angel! And that is the most comforting and beautiful thing of all. Thank you so much. You have no idea how much I needed that the past few years in watching her go."

Reflection: I have seen Reiki sessions bring so much comfort to people, which is another huge reason I continue to do it. I am so grateful to be of help to those who are open to receive the messages. I know that the client has to be ready or the messages won't come. I have gotten many messages for this client as she is so inclined to want to know more.

I always ask three times if I am supposed to give the message. And even then if I have doubts about it, the message will continue to be downloaded into my head until I agree to say it. Just like when there is an urgent place I need to go to, it just keeps replaying in my head. And when I need to move to a different part of the body when giving Reiki, I keep getting the message. My guides know it has to be beyond crystal clear for me to listen. It is the way I know, without a doubt, I should be doing what they are telling me.

February 2015

A client is going through a divorce. The emotional impact is high, as she tells me her story and cries. She wants to move forward but didn't know how to forgive. I told her to write a letter to him. Thank him for all the blessings she had with him, say good bye and burn it. She didn't know how that would help. I asked her, "IF he understood how you really felt, how it hurt you, would he have done it?" "No," she said. I told her "then you can forgive him. There was something off, not connected in his head where he didn't understand. He was in this relationship for financial gain, and you were in it for love. It was never going to work. You have the opportunity to grow your life any way you want to now. And you will find someone to love you for you." I gave her a half hour Reiki treatment on only the heart chakra to remove negative energy and replace it with loving cells. I got the message to ask her who says "You'll be fine Honey?" She laughed and told me she tells herself that all the time. She hugged me at least three times before leaving in a calm, peaceful state of mind.

March 2, 2015

Reiki Master Class

Tonight we were talking about entities that can attach to you. I was reading out of Diane Stein's book: <u>Psychic Healing</u> when all of a sudden I felt I was going to vomit. I had NO warning, I was reading mid-sentence and it hit me. I didn't physically vomit, but I could not get rid of the feeling, I kept swallowing trying to relieve the pressure. I went to the bathroom, returned with a drink and one of the Masters smudged me with white sage. I was so grateful they had the presence of mind to think of this, as I was not capable of thinking of it. I asked them to end class early and once they left I looked at my cell phone. I got a text from another client "Please send Reiki when you have a chance." I texted back "I was in Reiki Master class until now, are you ok?" The answer: "There is a lot of negative energy around, but something just released. I was at it for several hours. At the same time I was sending you Reiki and asking for help." I responded, "Wow, what time did you send me Reiki?" "About 20 minutes ago" This was, of course, why I had this feeling. I helped her pass the entity when she subconsciously asked for my help, I would say yes. I know that's what happened, and I felt like a wet noodle. Was it coincidence that I was teaching this exact topic when this occurred?

It taught me a huge lesson as I was ready for the shift to a higher vibration. I purchased a black tourmaline mala necklace of 108 beads. I wear this constantly while giving Reiki sessions or classes. It absorbs negative energy for me. I feel like it is my personal shield from negative energy or low vibrational entities or intrusions. They are out there looking for light, and they will attach to anyone who is not protected. This client had no idea what issues would happen to me simply by asking me to help. I had no idea that it was possible either, until that experience. I know that the person I helped needed it, and I am grateful I could be of assistance, even though I don't want that to ever happen again. This is something I have been close to experiencing in the past, but not to this extreme. Normally, I do feel nausea when there is an issue, but not like this.... I had to call upon St. Germaine and his violet flame to clear me before bed. I ask that all energies that are not mine leave or go back from where they came. I sometimes do this multiple times a day as I seem to pick them up everywhere. The grocery store, mall, work, everyone can have them!

Reflection: The more work you do with energy, the more you need to know about protecting yourself from negative energy.

Attachments can be found on people as you are giving Reiki. In one instance I remember a client saying she had a pain on the side of her hip and didn't know why. Once I felt it was an attachment I was able to ask her: "is there someone who feels attached to you at the hip?" She laughed and said "yes, my new assistant!" She said she recently traveled across country with her and was sitting next to her on a plane for several hours. It was during that business trip that the pain started. We had a conversation about how she could gain her own personal space back without feeling like she was abandoning her assistant. Our thoughts allow these negative energies into our system! This client wanted the new assistant to feel like a part of the family, opening herself up to the attachment. Once she agreed this needed to leave, I was able to ask her to use the selenite stick on the spot while I asked Archangel Michael to remove it with her. I continued to give her Reiki and when I knew Archangel Michael was done, I asked Archangel Raphael to come and fill in all the voids with loving new cells! In addition to the normally recommended bottle of water to drink, I also recommended the client take a salt shower when she got home to totally remove all negativity before going to bed.

Lots of times the energies in the location feel hard to me. I ask if it is an attachment mentally and can remove it with a selenite stick. Unless the client understands attachments, I don't tell them. Many people would be afraid or think I am crazy! As I hold the selenite stick in the spot where I feel the attachment is, I ask AA Michael to come with his blue sword and cut the attachment away. The attachments don't want to leave and I have to command them to leave by saying "In the name of God, you must leave (insert name of client here) now. Come into the selenite stick, and I will send you to God, who has more light than (name of client)". I then shake the selenite stick three times towards the window of the room as I ask God to bring the energy to the light. This typically needs to be done several times before all cords of attachment are finally cut with AA Michael. Once I know the attachment is gone, I ask AA Raphael to completely heal the area where the attachment had been and fill it in with love, before finishing Reiki. The client will feel lighter and physically different. Respect your selenite stick, thank it, smudge it (even though it is not necessary with this stone) and leave it in a window to recharge under a full moon before reusing. There are many ways to remove attachments, but this one works for me!

March 10, 2015

I stay at home to work as I have had nausea all am, from last night as well. My mom's nursing home calls, says she probably has a diverticulitis issue again and they put her on anti-biotics. The nurse tells me she was nauseous all night, and is in pain. I got off the phone and realized I am picking up on her physical ailment. I am concerned that she may be passing as I feel extremely weak 3 days before someone is going to pass, and I have been wiped out for two days already. I prayed to God to help her in any way she needs on her path now. I keep disconnecting cords, and trying hard to send love. To send unconditional love to her is difficult for me. I know it's her path, but she is my Mom. I pray when she does pass that I can get through it with love.

March 14, 2015

I get the call from the nursing home to tell me they are bringing Mom to the Emergency Room. I arrive before the ambulance and walk in with her. They do several tests, including a CAT scan, and say there is a bowel obstruction. She needs to be transferred to another hospital for surgery. Mom cries and she decided she is staying at this hospital to try meds, as she feels she's had this before, it will go away. In hind sight, I wonder if seeing the actual CAT scan would have made a difference in her decision. The medicine did help the swelling go down, as she looked nine months pregnant.

Over the years, my spirituality evolved from experiences from drum circles to angel classes to meditations and conversations with God on my own. Everyone who finds God does it in a multitude of ways, and it doesn't matter how you do it. Over the years I have witnessed my share of miracles, have felt the presence of angels and know the power of good over evil. I know how to invoke the angels and how to protect myself from negative energies. I never thought there were negative energies to protect myself from, and it shook me to my core when I finally experienced it.

One night I woke in the middle of the night with a pain in my left arm that radiated up into my heart chakra. I shook my husband and told him I thought I was having a heart attack. He asked if he should call an ambulance. I said get me a wash cloth and a glass of water. This was just enough time for me to compose my emotions so I could ask if this was my energy. "NO" was the answer. I grabbed my selenite stick and I saw (with my eyes closed- in the third eye) my mother. I said," Mom, is this you?" and she said "Yes." My husband was back with the water and he asked again "should I call 911" I said "NO, give me a minute" and he sat on the bed watching me. I turned my attention back to Mom and asked" what are you doing?" She said, "I am ready to die, I came to get you." I instantly replied, "I am not ready; you will have to go alone." She replied, "You said you would come with me. It's time." I told her "I don't know what I told you before, but I am NOT going now." I called Jesus to come and take her away. She yelled at me as Jesus had one arm under her arm pulling her along.

The selenite stick helped me keep her energy away from me. I keep it under my pillow all the time, and was grateful it was there tonight! As soon as Jesus left with her, the pain stopped. I had never felt anything like that in my ENTIRE LIFE! I was scared, sweating and worried about my life all at once. In as quick as you can read the above paragraph was how fast it actually happened. All my teaching Reiki in regards to being able to put aside the emotion was put into action. IF I was not able to do that one part, I am sure I would have been taken away to the hospital, probably for them to tell me it was stress. It makes you wonder how many people have experienced that same thing, and don't have the ability to intuit energy. It is a huge part of everyday life and something you need to understand so if and when it does happen you are ready.

Reflection: I still don't know why I was able to calm my feelings long enough to figure out if this was a real heart attack. My initial thought was to call an ambulance, but then I was able to pause long enough to determine if this was my energy. I am so grateful to my angels and the classes I have taken to know what to ask and when. Because of all the past times, in less intensity, that this happened, it prepared me for this event. I highly recommend calling an ambulance, as every second matters and this could have been life threatening.

I never thought that my Mom, who was still alive, could do such a thing. I had to remember that if I had this ability to intuit energy, she probably did as well. She never talked about it, but always claimed to "know that" before anyone else. She was always the one that everyone went to for answers to questions they had on their mind. I believe that we had a contract to die together, one that I needed to break through all times, past, present and future.

Sierra North helped me be by doing a soul retrieval drum meditation. We did it one night after a drum circle, and it was already late when we started at 9:30pm. We didn't leave until 11pm, and although it took time, it felt like five minutes. Sierra saw my mother with her hand in a cookie jar. The message was that she did it, but of course Mom would not admit it. Sierra did a releasing statement with me, and Sierra drummed and meditated as I sat in a chair next to her. The drumming was intense as she watched a jaguar dismember my whole body. She then watched Dr. Usui put me back together....once it was over, I felt like a wet noodle. I didn't see any of it, but energetically, I felt it. She instructed me to put a piece of black tourmaline and a piece of rose quartz in each corner of my bedroom. This was setting up a grid of energy to only allow loving energy into the room, and absorb any negative energy as soon as it got to my door.

In the weeks and months to come, Mom continued to return as she got closer and closer to passing. Each time I would hold the selenite stick, tell her I loved her, how sorry I was that I would not go with her and that she needed to get into the selenite stick, a light vehicle, to return to God who could give her all the love and healing she needed. There were times when I had to ask Jesus to come and get her as she would not leave me alone.

April, 2015

The past few months have taught me lessons of the heart. My Mom passed at the age of 92 ¾. We knew her time had come from the doctor explaining that without a colon operation, there was nothing more that could be done. I, of course, was all for the operation. I thought it would be simple enough; she will be fine as she is in decent health other than this one issue. I instructed the doctor to get us to the hospital and set it up. I then told Mom what my decision was and she said "I'm not going to have an operation." She stopped me in my tracks. "What do you mean Mom, this is simple, and they can fix it." "No, I will die on the operating table; I am not having an operation." No matter what I said after, it just made it worse. When she started to cry, I knew I had over stepped my authority. Then I started to cry, and just blurted out, "Mom, if you don't do this, you will die." She said, "You know I have to die sometime, how long do you think I am going to live?" "100," I said without hesitation. She just shook her head.

Throughout my entire life I have believed that everyone has their own path to live. No amount of logic or love of another is enough to change it. I had finally come face to face with my belief and had to acknowledge this truth. Even if it was my own mother! She was teaching me free will, the hard way.

I believe that every soul knows when it is going to die. Most people don't get to decide how or when they will die, but I felt like she did. Or maybe her intuition was just open enough to understand this in a way I had not yet. I kept thinking she should just have the operation, why is she being so stubborn? Why is she putting me through this emotional upheaval?

One of her nephews came to visit while she was at the hospital. His mom had died just after heart surgery, which was where my mom's fear came from. He totally understood her natural fear and helped me be more comfortable with her decision. After a week in the hospital trying everything but the surgery, she decided it was time to go back to the nursing home. She had lived here almost 10 years and wanted to see her stuff and the people she knew. With little food or liquid in her system, she started to deteriorate even more a week later. The hallucinations began and scared me more than I thought they could, even after reading about this on the internet. It was for a reason, of course. She was seeing scary people in her room, and it made her scream at the top of her lungs, which was why I was scared. I had NEVER seen her like this. My Reiki training made me reach for her rosary and put it in her hand, with mine over hers. Together, we held it up to where the scary people were sitting and told them, "in the name of Jesus, you must leave if you are NOT of the light." We said it three times and she looked at me and said, "How'd you know how to do that?" "I don't know," I said, "I just did." She was smiling for a few minutes. I told her any time they come back, you say it again. I put the rosary around her neck and told her to leave it there as a protection necklace. "OH, now I understand why the other ladies wear it around their neck," she was happy to have Jesus protecting her! The scary people were back within minutes and we did it again. Another time she was able to see a line of women walking by her room. She asked me where they were going, and I told her I didn't know, she should ask them. "Where are you going lady?" she yelled out. They replied they just walked up a mountain to get here, and they asked her to join. Mom said she's not going, as she thought they were going to the nurses' desk. Finally I told her they were angels, and this comforted her. I told her to listen to them; they may have something to tell her. She strained hard to hear them; there was a different way to hear than with just her ears. This was a distant gaze that looked so concentrated, like there was nothing else in the world that mattered. I wondered why I couldn't see or hear them. It would have been an amazing ability to share with her. She also told me a little girl was also in her bed, and she told her not to be afraid, that she would protect her. I tried hard to get mom to understand they were here to help her, not harm her. Once that sank in, I talked to the doctor who said this was "normal" but she could also have an infection, so they cleared that up. It was about 10 days of these hallucinations, and I thought I had lost my mom mentally.

Reflection: I often wonder if the medicine that she was given for her "infection" was causing the hallucinations. Either way, it gave me a new insight on protection necklaces for those in the final stages of life.

Then one day I went in and she was fully dressed sitting in her favorite chair. She had no idea what day it was and was shocked that she had lost so many days. The last thing she remembered was being at the hospital, which she thought was just another room at the nursing home. This clarity had given me renewed hope and I didn't leave her side much that day. I thought: if this is the last day, I want to talk to her as much as possible. She wanted to call my son, so I got out the cell phone and she told him "I just want to tell you I love you, and that love is all that matters. It's not about the money, if you aren't happy with whom you're with, find someone else. Life is short and you deserve to be happy." There were a lot of tears on that phone call. We reminisced about her younger years and all the fun she had in her life. She said it was a good life, and that's all that really mattered. It made me want to slow everything down, and stay in this moment. Her words of wisdom were awesome that day.

Reflection: Everyone hears these words of wisdom: life is short, be happy, love is all that matters. But do we DO IT? All too often we get stuck in our current comfort level and believe that is all there is for us. God wants the very best for everyone, so why not take a leap of faith to get what you want? Use Reiki on yourself daily and ask for what you want, be open to seeing the signs and move when the opportunity is available. You don't want to be on your death bed thinking what if I did _____ instead, would I have been happier, or experienced true love?

The next day, she was back in bed never to get up again. She would drift in and out of sleep and all we did was feed her ice chips for days. I could not understand HOW she was living on such little liquid. The Reiki in me decided to see if her chakras were closing down, so as she slept I took the time to find out. I knew the root was closed, and now the sacral and solar were as well. She decided I needed to take things home. She would tell me which drawer to go through and we would look at everything, talk about it and then decide what to do with it. A lot of things went to good will, and most were kept because "it's going to be worth money someday." Her Elvis collection, Yankee and Jeter memorabilia and pictures were worth more to me now than "someday". They embodied her passions and funny as they were to me, that's who she was.

The people at the nursing home came in one by one and said good-bye. She made them say it actually. She would tell them, "pray that I die soon." Some would say, "No, you'll be fine." She would look at them and say, "No, I am dying, pray for me." It didn't bother me too much until a deacon who she knew came in one day to pray with us. As we all held hands and he asked the Lord to comfort us, tears just rolled down my cheeks. I couldn't stop crying. I kept thinking how senseless this was, it didn't have to be this way; all she has to do is have the operation!!! I was angry with her.

That night, maybe because of all the tears, it finally came to me. Throughout my entire life, I have believed that everyone has their own life to live and path to follow. No amount of logic or love from another can change it. I had finally come face to face with my belief and had to acknowledge this truth and let her go. She was teaching me the life lesson of free will. At 92 ¾ quarters years old, I couldn't make her have the operation. I had to honor her free will to decide if she lived or died. I didn't like this experience, but I had no choice. Love never interferes with free will. I believe that is who God is, LOVE. Now I had to be like God, and let her decide. This was the hardest lesson I ever had to learn, and it took me 51 years to learn it.

Over the years, it was easier to let other friendships dissolve as I realized they needed to live on their own path. That old saying of being in someone's life for a season or a reason always was able to bring me to a logical understanding of WHY our friendship ended as it did. This was no different, yet because it was my Mom, I had to be able to put my emotions aside to look at it objectively. I had to love my Mom enough to let her decide. I had to love God enough to trust that this is her path, and have faith to know it's meant to be this way. I didn't have to fix it, just let her go and let God handle it. I remembered the Reiki principal, just for today I will honor my parents. This brought peace to my soul, and calm to my heart.

There were several days when I was bracing myself for her to pass. And then the next day would come and she would say, "Why am I still here?" My response was "Because it's called Divine timing, not your timing." Part of me wonders if I got my impatience from her! Then I could feel death looming. As the time came when I knew she would pass in a couple of days, I could NOT go and see her. As cold as it sounds, I was more afraid of the energy loss issues that could happen to me and I could not be there for her transition. I know she was waiting for me to be there, and I cried over it many days after that, but I just couldn't be there. I hope that she forgives me, even now.

My Dad's birthday came and I thought he would come and take her. When it didn't happen, I broke down in tears, pleading with him to come for her! I personally couldn't handle the stress even one more day! He came, the very next day. If I ever doubted he could hear me, it was now gone. Dad's birthday was April 17th and I believe Mom just wanted to be with him so bad. The morning of the 18th I used my gold sheen black obsidian to ask if Mom would pass today. As I looked into the gold sheen for pictures, I saw an angel holding a baby. Then the message I got was it was Archangel Michael (also known as the angel of death) and Mom....I cried uncontrollably, for a long time. I was happy that Archangel Michael was there with her, I knew there was nothing more I could possibly ask for, she was in the best hands now. I guess she didn't want to pass on Dad's birthday, so she waited just one more day. Her favorite nurse, Jennifer, was with her, holding her hand when she passed. I have a new appreciation for her and nurses' in general. She is my hero. I would not have been able to be there, to let her go, I had to be home, and let God and Jennifer handle it. Looking back, I often think I should have been a grown up and just suck it up and be there with her. But at the time, it was excruciatingly difficult. After all that I had been through, a small part of me still thought she wanted me to die with her. And although I am still here physically, a part of my heart is absolutely with her. As the days go by, she is in my daily thoughts as prayers, and signs of feathers show up to let me know she is near. Her spirit seems more attentive to wanting to help me now, even more so then when she was here. It makes me nervous as she seems different than when she was here....no longer a mom, more of the friend that I was searching for before she passed. I believe I am connecting with her heart now, something that was almost impossible in life.

Reflection: this reminds me of the story: A Piece of My Heart, that I have in the back of my Reiki 1 Practitioner book. I can't read it without crying!

One day a young man was standing in the middle of the town proclaiming that he had the most beautiful heart in the whole valley. A large crowd gathered and they all admired his heart for it was perfect. There was not a mark or a flaw in it. Yes, they all agreed it truly was the most beautiful heart they had ever seen.

The young man was very proud and boasted more loudly about his beautiful heart. Suddenly, an old man appeared at the front of the crowd and said "Why, your heart is not nearly as beautiful as mine."

The crowd and the young man looked at the old man's heart. It was beating strongly, but it was full of scars. It had places where pieces had been removed and other pieces put in, but they didn't fit quite right and there were several jagged edges. In fact, in some places there were deep gouges where whole pieces were missing.

The people stared -- how can he say his heart is more beautiful, they thought?

The young man looked at the old man's heart and saw its state and laughed.

"You must be joking," he said. "Compare your heart with mine. Mine is perfect and yours is a mess of scars and tears."

"Yes," said the old man, "yours is perfect looking but I would never trade with you. You see, every scar represents a person to whom I have given my love - I tear out a piece of my heart and give it to them, and often they give me a piece of their heart which fits into the empty place in my heart, but because the pieces aren't exact, I have some rough edges, which I cherish, because they remind me of the love we shared."

"Sometimes I have given pieces of my heart away, and the other person hasn't returned a piece of his heart to me. These are the empty gouges -- giving love, is taking a chance. Although these gouges are painful, they stay open, reminding me of the love I have for these people too, and I hope someday they may return and fill the space I have waiting. So now do you see what true beauty is?"

The young man stood silently with tears running down his cheeks. He walked up to the old man, reached into his perfect young and beautiful heart and ripped a piece out. He offered it to the old man with trembling hands. The old man took his offering, placed it in his heart and then took a piece from his old scarred heart and placed it in the wound in the young man's heart. It fit, but not perfectly, as there were some jagged edges.

The young man looked at his heart, not perfect anymore but more beautiful than ever, since love from the old man's heart flowed into his. --- Author Unknown

May 31, 2015

I decided to have an angel communication class to learn how to communicate with your angels and guides. I hoped and prayed that Mom would show up for me. Four ladies attended and although it was a good class for them, I had no communication from Mom. As I cleaned up after they left I got a text from Jennifer, Mom's nurse. She said:

"Sorry so late but I just wanted to let you know your mom is making her presence known here loud and clear!!! Her bed is still empty and well... her call bell light has been going on and off all night!!! We are all saying hi to her as the night goes on!! Wanted to let you know she's here!!"

I had not communicated with Jennifer since Mom's funeral, and she certainly had NO IDEA that I was having a class that night. I sent back: "OMG!!! I just ended a communicating with your angel's class that started at 6pm. It's been 42 days today that she passed, I am not surprised! She knows we are waiting for signs, and I know they will be coming a lot now!"

Jenn said: "We tried everything to fix it, nope...she's still making it go off!"

I finally told Jenn that she must have a message for you, to ask her. She did and she thought it was confirmation to her to leave that job....where ever Jenn ends up, we are now lifetime friends!

Reflection: Around Mothers' Day a year later, a light in my kitchen flickers on and off. I have to pay attention to what is going on or being said and recognize she is with me even when I don't believe it is true.

My mother's passing put a shift into everything I've been doing with A Hand in Healing. The healing is needed, yet I don't feel a need to constantly hold classes. I will always give Reiki sessions and teach Reiki, but I want to do more. I thought about how my obituary would read. I don't want it to say I owned A Hand in Healing….yeah, and? The people who were healed there would remember me for what I did, but I want to make a bigger impact. I decided that I needed to tell people these stories so that others could learn, and grow from them. They can't just die with me. Other books tell you how to do Reiki, I wanted my book to share the results of Reiki and other amazing healing modalities!

July 25, 2015

About year or two ago a client's family member had issues moving his right arm. The client asked me to send the family member (FM) Reiki and FM agreed to distance Reiki. I asked FM what was wrong and was told FM was deeply depressed. At this point we didn't know a diagnosis and I told the client the FM was very depressed. The client told me I had it totally wrong, that Reiki was false. I apologized and never said another word about it. Months later, FM was diagnosed and the client approached me and said you were right, FM is depressed. When I found out about it, I assembled a bag of stones for FM's healing and offered Reiki. FM didn't want any touching so FM just requested distance Reiki. When I sent it I found FM was having a hard time connecting to God. I told FM all that was needed was to ask God for what was wanted. A strange look of fascination came over his face. I explained to FM that a conversation about health and what achievements were wanted in life is acceptable. This gave FM comfort, as I saw a smile appear.

This week FM's gallbladder had to be removed and the air from the surgery has not dissipated from the body fast enough. The air has moved the FM's diaphragm making it harder to breathe than normal. The client told me this and I mentioned that the hospital offers Reiki, all they have to do is Reiki under the breastbone with one hand and put the other one over the stomach area. The next thing you know, I am invited to go give him Reiki on Saturday. I hesitated as part of me knows that they don't believe in Reiki, and yet I feel for FM's soul, I need to be there. I never charge for this service, as I know the people really need it. I asked my guides what I needed, and brought selenite, to remove the negative energy. I had an assortment of other stones and my dragon statue for extra energy. When I got there I set up all the stones in chakra order facing his bed, and placed a flower of life painting by Kasey Gordon under his bed. I explained I was first going to remove any negative energy from his room. Then I set up a gold protection bubble over the entire room and asked my guides to come and help. Archangel Michael is there to protect but also helped me remove the negative energy and stale air that was in the diaphragm area. It was intense; my hands were sweating as I asked that any negative energy come into my hands to be recycled to mother earth as love. I was told we were removing fear of death. This is not why I thought I was here, but of course I do whatever is needed. I worked half an hour in one spot, at one point I was so hot, that I knew it was at a breaking point. I asked Archangel Raphael to heal it for me, and keep me upright as I was feeling faint. I could see and hear from the monitors that he was getting uncomfortable. My throat started to get a tickle and it wasn't long after that I asked the Archangels to continue the healing as we left the room for the nurse to come in.

A few days later I wake up with diarrhea, and am weak. This is the weak feeling I get when someone is about to pass. I pull myself together a few hours later to get to work. My client tells me that they have about 24 hours to decide if they will do a tracheotomy on the family member. I believe FM is ready to pass, and the feeling tells me he has about 3 days. At the end of Monday FM decided not to have the tracheotomy, the family is devastated. I am sooooo tired; sleep more than normal- 11 hours. Tuesday I wake up to the smell of frankincense and myrrh. I don't normally smell anything, so I make a mental note of it, and wonder what it means. I shower and get dressed and can still smell it on and off. As I drive to work it gets stronger and stronger as I am at my desk, the smell is almost constant. I am feeling tired and my legs are weak again and try to eat chocolate to bring my energy up....it doesn't work. By 1pm Tuesday, July 28, I get the email that says FM passed with his family holding on. The rest of the work day I kept praying that FM was with God. As I drove home, absolutely exhausted from the day, I am told the smell is to tell me Jesus was coming to get FM. I take comfort in that new knowledge. I can say I know 3 days before when someone is going to pass. The energy is distinct in my body and I now understand that no amount of sugar or sleep is going to change the outcome, I have learned to go with the flow and do what my body tells me. Once the person passes, I start to return to "normal" and feel better within hours. I wonder why I have to feel weak, what is happening to my energy? Am I allowing the person who is passing to take some of it to finish their journey? I struggle with the knowledge of their passing and what to do with it. I am not going to walk around telling people about it, I hope that in some small way I could help him transition. Being an empath is difficult work. You can connect with people's emotions and although you can't change any of it, the idea is to be able to get them to understand there is hope, love and healing for everyone. No matter what vibrational level they need it at, no matter what your life has been or your beliefs previously were, up until now.

Reflection: While giving Reiki to someone in person or distance, if I feel their soul is getting ready to pass, I set up a pillar of light next to them. I explain during distance Reiki that this light pillar goes directly to God. Your soul can use it any time, multiple times to "chat" with God. It is not for me to understand what the process is, just to be able to give them tools to start their communication with God. It is very hard to have honest conversations about what is going on in the subconscious mind of anyone. Most generally, I do not tell people what information I am receiving as they really don't want to know. In this case and others, the only reason I did tell is because they were so desperate to know what was happening. My relationship with the person has a lot to do with whether I reveal this information. I believe a lot of people still think this work is not to be taken seriously until they experience it for themselves. Telling them unsettling information is not something that I do quickly. There is a lot of thought into how it is said and when is the right time to reveal it. The reason I do it is to help them understand what is going on. It is in an effort to give them some comfort, and another way to think.

Reflection: I often think about the conversations I had when starting Reiki about being a soul healer, or soul developer. This is happening more and more now. I want people to be able to consider other options. There are always possibilities; the mind has to be able to weigh all options before deciding the right one. Sometimes you are so caught up in a past belief or limited understanding that you can't comprehend any other way. Leading people to God is never a bad option. If this is all I do, I am honored to be able to help.

I follow Doctors with Reiki on twitter and he published <u>Divine Healing Codes and How to Use Them</u> on Friday June 13, 2014. I did not see them until a day or two before my client's family member passed on July 28, 2015. I wish I had known about them sooner! These codes 'come through' from Divine Mother, Archangel Raphael, and Source. There is a numeric code for almost any disease you can identify and you simply write the number on your body daily for healing. I used these codes with Reiki on a man who had a stroke and is in a rehab facility. I gave his wife (who didn't use Reiki) the codes and asked her to continue using them on him daily. Four days later, she calls and says he was singing for the first time since the stroke more than two months ago. He was barely able to say a whole sentence before; I had chills as she told me nothing else had changed in his medicines or routine.

I use the codes routinely on issues I have, repeating the numbers or writing them on myself where the issue is continuously throughout the day. I ask God, Divine Mother, Archangel Raphael to come and heal me each time I use them. It makes sense to me that if a name has a vibrational number, then a disease would as well. Maybe there is a healing code for everything, and we just have not found them all yet!

A friend says her mom was up through the night, feeling sick. She started googling the codes and wrote down three codes on sticky notes, including one for insomnia. Within 15 minutes she was sound asleep and woke up in the am perfectly rested and feeling fine!

One lady was experiencing a migraine coming on and I wrote the code on a sticky note, placed it on her forehead and then gave her Reiki for 15 minutes, and the migraine was gone!

July 2015

A client texted me while she and her finance were at a car dealership. When she got such an awful vibe from the dealership, she started getting nervous. As they were test driving the car, she could not shake the feeling and asked what she could do. The dealership was starting to make a deal and she interrupted and said they needed to leave. Her finance said there's a bad vibe here and if she says we have to leave, we do.

I told her.....You need to be able to put your emotions aside to be able to ask some questions. It's hard, but important to figure out what is the best thing to do. You could have been picking up on the vibes of the person driving you around or it could have been the car. Think about when you first started feeling weird. Were you with the guy? Or, is it happening while you are with the car? Once you feel it, stop what you are doing and stand still and start asking questions. Why am I feeling this way? Is it me? Is it the guy? When you get one answer, continue with the next question. Keep going until you get the information you need to understand it. This takes time and practice to tune everyone out around you. This is your intuition telling you what you need to do. You can even ask questions before you leave. Is this the place to go to find the perfect car?

Reflection: Many people have bad vibes and think it's just them and brush it to the side. You are recognizing signs; the next step is to act on it by asking questions: What is this I am feeling? Why is this happening now? Listen to the answers and follow through on the advice you receive. Once you are through it how do you feel? Most of the time if you have listened, you feel fine on the other side of it. This is your intuition helping you get away from something that is not good for you. Trust it.

I am not sure when this happened, but somewhere in my Reiki journey I have learned compassion for EVERY LIVING THING. Yes, this is a Reiki principal, and yet sometimes you read words, and they really don't resonate with you. Then, I heard it again when I went through the Munay-Ki Rites, and I thought to myself no way am I going to be nice to spiders. One day there was one that I just looked at and told it to leave. I then went outside the house and had a discussion with all the insects and bugs that they needed to stay outside in order to stay alive. NO insiders allowed, as I could not be certain of their life span inside the house. I felt ridiculous doing it, and yet, not one spider could be found for the entire season. Then it grew to include the people in my life that I could no longer see eye to eye with….I found new ways to let them leave. Instead of losing my control and sounding like the bad guy, I simply let them choose to leave. Then they thought they won, and I never had to break a sweat. Once you realize you will not get along with everyone in your life for your entire life, it's easier. You realize everyone is in your life for a reason, and once it's over, it's ok if they or you need to leave. For some it is easier to be angry when it happens so they feel validated. But another Reiki principal is just for today, I will not be angry. Sometimes I have to say it a lot for me to finally be calm. But now, I just want to remain calm and Reiki on.

September 7, 2015

The daughter of a client I know tells me her mom's surgery will be between 10 and noon. I said thanks, I was just thinking about her! I will be sending Reiki to last 24 hours in the am, and that should cover her! She has a strong connection to God, when I send Reiki, it is very clear that her relationship is very special.

Our text message reads:

Daughter says, "thank you – You are very special to be able to connect like this." I respond "You are sweet to say that but anyone can learn how! I sent Reiki at 10am, and again after noon, the Reiki is very weak right now, but I find that to be normal during surgery. I will send again around 4." I actually sent Reiki at 9pm, and felt she was resting comfortably. "I recommend you keep talking to her, as she can hear you even though she can't respond." Daughter said- "You are spot on, she had a restful night last night but this am her anxiety built up. She went in at 1:30 procedure started at 3, done at 6. They repaired the issue. She is one heck of a strong lady. Just before they took her, she said to me, I don't know what I'd do without you. I told her, don't worry about that, concentrate on your center self, tune into your energy. Told her this procedure will only make her stronger. You have been spot on with your energy. Thank you from the bottom of my heart." On September 9, I sent her a healing attunement; she was like a sponge soaking it in. Energy is so much better! This happened at a time when more love will flood the earth, she is ready to take it all in and give it to those who need it. She is beaming with love now. She is so appreciative of life; she makes me smile with tears in my eyes.

Reflection: I always do distance Reiki the same way. I think by sticking with what works I am able to quickly assess the session. I use my left hand and imagine the person lying with their head to the tips of my fingers and their feet at the end of the hand where it meets the wrist. The person's crown chakra is in the top section of finger up to where in bends. The second chakra is in the next section to where the knuckle bends. The third chakra is from the knuckle to the section where the finger meets the hand. The fourth chakra is just under the part where the index finger meets the hand and so on to the seventh chakra at the end of the hand where it meets the wrist. By knowing these are the chakras of the person, I know where the energy is going to them as I am sending them Reiki. I typically can figure out which chakra is the issue and then feel a pinch of pain on a section of my body indicating which organ I need to work on.

September 8, 2015

I received this message from Seraph Rose Aura during a Reiki session for a client today: It is the Earth chakra you are feeling bringing you down. Realize this must occur for unconditional love to flow even greater than ever. Take the time to connect with Mother Earth beneath you. Please realize your true worth on Earth is beyond material. Your connection to vibration is what is changing, bringing you to a higher calling. She showered you with love at each chakra, it was so beautiful! I could see hearts being put into each chakra....I never saw that before, so amazing!

September 10, 2015

A client has throat issues. Her Reiki session lead me to tell her she is holding back discussions when she should be saying things, for business and personal life. She applied to a church to be the Godmother of a child. She attended this church her whole life and now they denied her application because she is not in compliance with church rules. This rocked her emotions to the core. It made her finally verbalize her frustrations to the church. Life gives you what you need to heal. Are you listening to the messages your body is sending?

September 19, 2015

Since January, people have been passing –in my personal life and at my full time job, in record numbers. Twenty so far, more than I thought would occur, EVER in one year. For me, things have to happen a lot for it to make an impact and for me to learn a lesson from it.

I have been working on my heart chakra, since I found out I had anemia. I had to first struggle to get back my strength taking iron pills and diet change. Since then my heart chakra has been the main event. I find myself attracting clients with heart issues that need healing and am realizing this is my specialty. Two years into this and I can easily feel someone's hurting heart. It has made me more compassionate, because although we cannot always see people's hurts, I can feel it. Those who smile so much on the outside are often the ones who are hurting the most.

Reflection: People have to understand, first and foremost that every individual has a life plan. That means each person has their own individual thing to accomplish. WE don't know what that is. It is between each person and their God. For us to mourn the loss of loved ones is understandable. However, we need to be able to take the lessons learned with love and keep going on our own path. I especially like helping people in this "stuck" area. It is so important to be able to move on. You never forget the love of the person in your life, you take that with you. It even makes you stronger as you have an angel watching over you, protecting, guiding and continuing to love you from heaven.

September 20, 2015

8:30pm I smell frankincense. This tells me someone is passing. I KNOW it is a family member that has been ill and I sit to send distance Reiki. The family member tells me it is the body that gives out, and then the soul agrees it is time to leave. Interesting because that is not something I would have thought of, nor considered, yet seems obvious now. This family member fought hard, against medical issues that are so rare, there may be medical texts about it. He is just here now tying up ends for those he is leaving behind. I asked that I not be woken for help in the middle of the night, as I am tired. Over 20 people have died since the beginning of the year and I am tired of crying, and not being to help heal everyone.

Reflection: I have yet to realize that the work I am doing is helping, just not to the extent I anticipate. I have to remind myself to put my ego aside and know that the person gets what they need. I don't know what they need; I just have to trust in God. And of course, I do trust God. Maybe I just don't always trust that what I am giving is the most I can give. I always wonder: did I miss something, should I have done more?

September 26, 2015

I ask a person in the Reiki Master class to come and give me Reiki. I don't ask very often as I generally want to heal myself, but today I don't have the strength, as I have been trying for an entire week to heal this sciatica pain. Although the session went very well, the pain did not go away. I can't figure out why I have it, but I take a nap during the day, sometimes you just have to give in and go with the flow. Later in the day, I find out that my family member passed early in the am today. It's 10pm and I connect with my family member with distance Reiki. He tells me he had a blood clot in the right leg, where I felt the pain. He helped me clear and repairs all RNA/DNA issues in our family line from past, present and future generations so no one will go through what he endured. I feel horrible that I didn't want to help him, although I did set up a pillar of light for him to be able to talk to God. I realize that as a healer, this is who I am, and there is no time clock to punch. I have to work when people say they need help now. I vow never to do that again, and pray for his safe return home. I found it interesting that he passed the day before the Lunar eclipse. This has been said to be where wave "X" hits planet Earth to bring us from the third to fifth dimension.

Reflection: The 5th dimension is where there is no ego left, only love for each other. As I do more and more work talking to family members who have passed, all I feel is the love. They want us to heal the grief of missing them and realize they are with us to bring us to a higher vibrational energy field. They know the challenges we face and are still just a thought away from helping us. All we have to do is ask, and they will help comfort us.

A Reiki Practitioner sent me this text:

"It's hard to explain but I feel there is something calling to me but I'm not connecting with it. I felt it after Reiki 1 class, but not very strong. Then, in the last couple of weeks it's been getting strong. Taking Reiki 2 class feels right to find out what is calling me". I respond: "That's how it happens; you get the calling and just know it's the right path for you now." She replies: "After I sent the text, I felt relief and anticipation. As if the energy was saying you figured it out! And now you're on your way with your journey! What a feeling! I said, Yes, it just gets better, deeper, move overwhelmingly beautiful!"

Reflection: This kind of situation happens again and again on the Reiki path as your intuition expands and you listen to the inner self telling you what you should be doing. This is a beautiful part of life. If this is all that Reiki does for you, it is more than enough to bring you the peace you have been searching for, and it's right inside you! You have heard the phrase, "Go Within." Reiki helps you do it!

September 28, 2015

I used to be sad for each person who passed. The grief would grip me for days, my heart so consumed with sadness for those left behind. I think about my mother who got to a point where she honestly wanted to start her continuation day. Just as much as I wanted her to live, she wanted to die. I finally got to a place of understanding that, and once I did, it was ok to let her go. For if that is truly what she wanted for her soul, who am I to stop her? Yes, it's heartbreaking that she is no longer here. I am being selfish. Once I came to understand that emotion, I could let her go.

What's left? The love. The memories. The reason they made you who you are today. Once you are here, FOCUS on it. Intently. Stay in the LOVE. This new revelation pushed me forward to teach everyone else the same lesson. This came from years of allowing me to feel the emotions, not pushing them down. Years of sending distance Reiki and connecting with their beautiful souls. Listening to their advice on what their bodies are telling them. It's another reflection on becoming a Reiki Master. Each time, you think you got it, there's another layer to explore. Reiki is constantly changing my heart to be closer to God.

Reflection: This is why my mother was able to stay here without any food or water so long. My energy was keeping her here, until I learned the lesson. This is why we say there are so many layers to healing. If you haven't broken down in tears, you probably haven't learned the lesson yet.

September 30, 2015

I wake up to this in my head: "Everyone. Everyone. Everywhere. Everywhere. The time has come to give you the secret to healing the mind." I ask "Should I get up and write this down?" "Yes"

I get out of bed, walk cross the house and turn on lights hoping this "voice" is not going to leave while I struggle in the dark to find my pad and a pen. Without my glasses on I just write and hope I can read it in the am.

"For centuries you sit in a room to meditate. The secret is to go within. Take the time to be alone, be it in nature or in a room. You need the silence of mind to give you the answers within. Go to sleep with a sizeable fluorite, ask from the heart and soul for the answer to a question. Write it down when you get the answer in the middle of the night. We want to communicate with you. We want you to learn. This has been done for centuries, it cannot hurt you. Please try it. We want to support you."

I ask this question: How did Jesus heal others so quickly?

"Come from the heart, with the third eye, see the person bathed in love, washed in golden light, cleansed of all issues, by the grace of God. You must carry the love in your heart before you are able to do it. All healing comes from love. This shift to 5D brings you there faster. You need to be here to experience miraculous healings. EVERY TIME. STRIVE TO BE LOVE. Love is all you need. Any time you are not love, take a moment to remember and ask for it to return. Ask Jesus, he will come instantly. Be Love. Once you know the peaceful feeling in your heart, you yearn for it more and more. This is the shift to 5D. This calm, peaceful loving feeling is where you need to be to heal all things; body, mind and spirit.

As you shift, it is natural to lose things, fear is one. You are at peace in 5D. There is no place for fear when in love. Strive to get here when you feel fear come on. You will get here faster. Think love, come from your heart space, feel it calm you, know Jesus' love within. Be love. BE LOVE needs to take over your mind to feel it in your heart. Let this be your mantra. BE LOVE. Very simple, yet complete. Be Love. From this frame of mind all is good. You find good in all. If love is your path, blessings, healings are yours. Be love. What would love do? The answer to all your questions comes from here. Be love. Radiate it out from all you do, be love. The peace is within. This calm is where you need to come from. Be love. Use symbols to heal: heart and cross. Blow in where needed, in gold. You see the heart in Jesus statues for this reason, love is all you need. Come from the heart, everyone, everywhere." AA Gabriel

I can't explain the feeling of calm and love that came with these words. Reading them now doesn't do it justice, as the feeling can't be described with detail. Each time "Be Love" was said, it was as if it was a meditation making me go deeper into the love. Incredibly soothing, unlike any other meditation I have ever felt!! I have been trying to work with AA Gabriel for a little while now, and so glad I am making a connection! This was a very personal message, and my heart is so grateful!

I was also told to use symbols to heal; heart and cross. Blow them in where needed, in gold. I believe the reference was to the statue that you commonly see with Jesus' heart in gold. I heard, "Come from the heart, heal with love." During my entire Reiki life, I often wondered about whether Jesus used Reiki or some higher powered form of it. I believe Jesus, and all deities, have a healing power. What it is called may not be something we ever really understand. Connecting to your God and or deity is all that matters. Once you have that soul connection, there is nothing you can't accomplish together.

Reflection: This was the first time Archangel Gabriel gave me a message. I tell you the difference between writing my own words and his are the quickness and grace of the flow of words. It was as if Archangel Gabriel was in the room speaking and I was taking notes. Archangel Gabriel spoke slowly enough for me to write it down, yet fast enough to just keep me writing without stopping or looking up. As I was writing, I understood the words to put them on paper but I was concentrating on writing the words and really didn't understand the message until it was over and I was able to reread it. Love is all you need comes to light again. This one message is drilled into my head over and over.

October 1, 2015

I give Reiki to a beautiful dog that was in a car accident and had her rear right leg amputated. She gets along amazingly well for a dog missing a leg. She greeted me as if she knew me forever, didn't even bark as was expected from her owner. I had to immediately put down my bags and begin giving her Reiki. She just soaked it all in. We gradually moved from the floor to a couch where she could not get closer to me. Her head on my chest with her nose to my mouth; it was as if she was trying to inhale me! Dogs and animals are amazing; they are so innocent and trusting of Reiki energy. When I was done almost 45 minutes later, she simply walked away. I explained how important I thought it would be for her owner to be able to give her Reiki on a daily basis. I have a feeling the owner will take the class, and find the beautiful changes all around her as well!

October 5, 2015

I was asked to send distance Reiki to a client who was having surgery. I had met this lady previously and knew of her spirituality and love of natural healing. Several days I sent Reiki, including the day of surgery, and knew she would come out of surgery fine. Her connection to God was so strong, I just knew there was more she needed to do here, to teach her family. Four weeks later I was asked to go see her at her house for Reiki. I learned that for years she would go to Herkimer NY and dig for Herkimer diamonds. She had, in my opinion, a beautiful obsession with them. They were everywhere, outside and inside the home, and she even gifted me with a gorgeous Herkimer diamond drusy cluster. She showed me a gorgeous necklace she had, and I just knew she was supposed to wear it. I put it on her and told her she needed to wear it to continue to heal. I asked her what she needed today, and she said she wanted to remove toxins from her body as she knew her body was not "right".

I gave her a Reiki treatment, with heart shaped stones for each chakra. I called Seraph Rose Aura to help when I got to the heart chakra. The energy here was steady, but purposely NOT intense. Seraph Rose Aura told me that, and she continued to work on her while I completed the session. When I was done she asked me why this happened. I gave her a book on the soul's purpose in hopes it would answer some of her questions. My client told me about her mom who died young from the same issue she just had surgery to "mend" as she called it. I told her about the fact that Wave "X" just came through about the same time that she had this done. Raising the vibrations from 3rd dimension to 5th, bringing people out of ego into love. I thought that it was interesting, the timing of her surgery with the love dimension. Her husband then came in with a huge Herkimer Diamond which he had gifted her years earlier. I cleared it and infused it with Reiki before putting it on the floor on the side of her bed, and instructed her to leave it there for additional energy. I left feeling blessed to have been able to have the time we shared.

The next day I look up the metaphysical properties of Herkimer Diamond, because something is nagging at me. OF COURSE!!! IT REMOVES TOXINS AND HEALS DNA! I instantly text that to the family and advise them to keep the Herkimer's around her all the time. They text back in a few hours saying she is being rushed to the hospital. They ask for advice, and it hit me. The client needs to ask her Mother to come and help her heal this DNA issue now. All these years have led her to this time, when she has all the natural elements all around her to do it. The Herkimer's are there to heal her and the DNA of the family. THIS IS HER SOUL PURPOSE! She returns home that evening, with new information on why she is here...exactly what she asked for, and received!

I use stones in every session but the very first one. I want the client to feel Reiki without stones first. In the above case, this lady had been using Herkimer Diamonds for years, and she was thrilled to be able to have them help her heal her DNA. More and more I am noticing those who are accepting of Reiki are healing family DNA. This is huge in the way future generations will live and die.

October 11, 2015

I was very disappointed that Reiki did not work on my hip/right leg pain. Sierra sent Reiki on October 9 and said I had an attachment, which she removed. She told me all I had to do was to continue to Reiki it with soothing light. I used a selenite stick on it every chance I could get and it would take it away. Then when I didn't have the stone on it, it would return. My conversation turned to God/Jesus: "Why can't I heal myself? I am a Reiki Master, teaching people. I wonder if this is why people stop teaching. Do they get pain that they can't get rid of? I understand we are mere mortals, not Gods. What am I missing? Is it a lack of faith? Do I need more faith? How do I get it? Are there different levels of faith? Is this another test of my patience?"

I called Sierra North, she stopped on the side of the road to do a distance healing with me over the phone for over an hour. I released my contracts with any soul or person who thinks I was supposed to be their salvation and released all fear and guilt that I didn't help everyone heal. With over 20 people passing this year, I have to realize that although I can feel their pain, sympathize with their love of life and people around them; it is not my responsibility for what happens. It is between them and God. NOT ME. I can be a facilitator of healing, a comforter to those around them. It is NOT my place to judge them or myself as a bad healer. We all have a path; my "power" will be in having a safe place where people can find me. My passion is in teaching Reiki so they can find the power within them to heal. Healing truly is from within. And in times when you doubt you have it, you have to take time off to dig deeper and reconnect again. That's where your faith is, within. I had to reconnect with my soul, inner child, to give her permission to get rid of any attachments from all those who had attached to me. Part of healing is reaching another layer of emotion that is preventing the healing from taking place. I had to put in the work myself. This is why all this happened, to make me move to a higher vibration. It normally gets harder right before it gets easier. I am guessing that is what is happening now.

Reflection: It made me realize, the heart holds all of our emotions.... rage, anger, fear, love, joy, sadness, grief, sorrow, loneness. Letting them out appropriately is the part no one tells you how to do. When done effectively, you recognize the emotion, and release it to God as something he can heal for or with you. It is not something you have to hold onto, nor is it good for your mind, body, spirit to do so. If you are holding onto it, this is when disease happens. Release it by vocalizing it, writing a letter or share with a Reiki Master, friend or professional who can help you move on. You need to know when your body needs help and stop to work on it. Don't push it aside, thinking it can wait. If you are having emotions that are bothering you, this is your inner child reaching out for help. Listen, do something. You will feel better and your soul will be happy. The Reiki journey is hard.

You question why you signed up to do this work. The answer is because even if during just one Reiki session, you share your hope with healing, change their faith in themselves, or help them realize the connection to their God, that light may be what your client needs to propel them on their soul path! THAT is the Divine working through you. And THAT is enough. Blessings to you on your Reiki journey!

October 18, 2015

I feel like someone is dying for the past 3 days. Today, I have zero motivation, very tired, and just want to sleep. It's Sunday and spitting snow outside. I think about the first time we saw snow after Dad died on April 8, 1995. It was spring, doing this same type of freaky snow storm. I remember sitting at the kitchen table with Mom and thinking this was Dad's way of telling me he's in heaven. Then it hit me! Mom's now telling me she's in heaven with Dad. I start crying when I realize today is the six month anniversary since she passed. Now it all made sense. I was seeing the snow on this date, feeling weak....it all connected for a reason. I just had to figure it out!

Reflection: Be sure to give yourself time to make connections. Your body is first to shout out to you and get you to listen. Dates are important and if your mind doesn't remember, your subconscious mind will, just take the time to be still and listen.

The topic of healing from within returns again in November when a client is having knee issues. She would Reiki it, it would go away and come back. She got aggravated with Reiki not working, threw up her hands and decided to go back to taking medicine. When I sent her Reiki, I got the message that she really does want to heal it naturally, but doesn't want to put the time into making it work. I asked her I AM Presence where she needed to give herself Reiki, and was told the solar plexus. The WILL is what needs attention. AH HA! When I told her this in person, it made perfect sense to her. She needed to will it to happen, and she had not given it the attention it needed. This mantra was given to me for her to repeat:" I AM healthy, whole, well and complete that I AM." She decided to make an effort and really concentrate on healing it that night. The very next day she reported not having to use a cane, and she began a new focus on taking the time needed to heal it with Reiki daily. I explained that this knee issue appeared so she would understand that she can heal herself if that is her focus. Too many times people put their belief in another's hand to heal them. True healing comes from within. Yes, it's time consuming, but ultimately worth it!

Reflection: Over the years, I have seen this over and over. Your healing is based on your intention. You must watch your thoughts and words, saying "It could be worse" does not help the healing. Reiki becomes part of all that you do, healing every part of you, including your vocabulary. Also take a look around your home and office, what words or paintings are displayed there? I once saw a picture of a sinking boat in a person's home. This is NOT the kind of energy you want around you if you are trying to heal!

A friend, Kathy C., comes for Reiki due to depression. Her brother, Bob A., took his own life a short time ago. She was upset that he didn't reach out to her for help. While on the Reiki table she asked her Mom, Dad and brother to come and see her. They did, and when she saw her brother Bob she asked him out loud, "why, why, why?" I heard Bob instantly start explaining to me through my mind. He had a soul contract with the woman he wanted to marry. He loved her more than anyone or anything he ever loved, and felt she was his soul mate. She had an affair and he found out. To teach her a lesson, he shot himself in the heart. She now deals with his death on a daily, second to second basis, it is completely overwhelming for her. The soul contract was set up to teach her of his unconditional love in this lifetime. It could have gone either way, if she understood it, she would have been with him until death. She didn't understand and needed to "be sure" and cheated, which broke his heart. In the next lifetime, should they agree to meet, she will know without a doubt, of his love for her. There was nothing Kathy could have done to stop this or help Bob. Kathy had a huge sense of peace and believed it was true.

When someone's loved one has passed, and they don't understand why God would take their loved one from them, Reiki may be able to help. If they hold onto the sorrow, it can put them in a depressed state of mind. Once it's in the mind, it can weaken the heart, body and soul. Some hold onto just one thing and they say: if only I had done _____, or I wish I had time to say _____. It plays over and over in their mind, each time causing more pain and anguish because they can't forgive themselves. What if during Reiki, you knew that they can hear you now? What if they know you love them? I know Reiki can provide that level of comfort, as I have seen it happen again and again. This is just starting to unfold here, and the peace of mind Reiki can provide is amazing!

I have been using the phrase "love is all you need" on Facebook a lot lately. I want people to understand that with LOVE anything and everything is possible. This morning I woke knowing that I need to implement that more in my own life. It is easy to say. However doing it is different. To be able to come from a place of love all the time, no matter what the situation takes an unbelievable amount of internal strength. No one sees that. It makes me realize that those who have it worked hard to get it. It's putting aside all emotion and letting the love take over. There is an intense amount of personal work involved. There is more listening and less talking, and then understanding comes from it. Love is a deep subject and I believe most people don't do the work to understand the unity with God it requires. Or, maybe the faithful have the unity and others struggle to find it outside themselves. Go within all the time, it is there just waiting for you. When love expands with in you there is a physical feeling. The heart chakra cracks, you can feel the tightening releasing. This is what occurs to let more love in. And then you can let more love out.

Christmas 2015

I get the gift I had forgotten I even wanted. SO happy to get a kindle! I purchase Anna, Grandmother of Jesus and began to read it the day after Christmas. It is a book you can't put down once you start and filled with so much information, I highlighted pages and pages of tips! This is the book I have been looking for, and am so overjoyed I finally found it, that I text everyone I know and tell them to buy it, they need to read it too! There are specific prayers to say, and it tells you HOW Jesus healed! Reading it made me understand that there is no way I will EVER be able to experience all the lessons Jesus learned. Just due to where we live, it is impossible to be able to do all the things required to have the same understanding. The main point of all of it is to heal with LOVE. I have experienced that over and over and now it is validated. My husband had a horrible sore throat and coughed so much one night I had to do something. I asked Jesus to sit in my heart and then I asked that God's white/gold light move through me and heal his throat. I had my hands above him a few inches but wasn't there even a minute and he stopped coughing. The next day I asked him if he felt a difference in my Reiki. He told me that my hands were too hot, and is why he moved away from me. Interesting enough, I didn't use any Reiki and my hands didn't feel hot to me at all. I think back to my Mothers' statue of Jesus pointing to his heart that has rays of light coming from it. The answer has been here all along, but I didn't see the connection until today!

A few days later a friend needs Reiki for her wrist. Her mom had carpel tunnel and she is now complaining of the same pain. I again used the "God's light" method with Reiki and worked on her wrist for about 15 minutes. Again, I only felt cold in her wrist. She said it immediately felt better and was able to use it more the next day. Through all these occasions I am noticing that God is now working through me. Back at the beginning of my training with Reiki, I honestly didn't think that was possible. Why would God pick me? Guess what? He picks ALL of US! EVERYONE can heal with his LOVE!

I have a get together with a few Reiki Masters and explain this concept is how Jesus healed. He asked God to help him. Jesus saw the person as perfect and allowed the light to flow through him to the person needing the healing. It is using LOVE as the healing ingredient! This concept allows me to look and see everyone differently now. I find myself sending LOVE with my eyes to everyone. At the gym, supermarket, bank, work, anywhere I AM, there is healing. It's miraculous! I finally understand the words I AM GOD.

Reflection: When I first learned Reiki, my hands would sweat a lot. I took it as a sign that Reiki was working and I knew when it stopped, I was done. After the Archangel Raphael attunement, my sensation in the hands felt deeper; still hot, not sweaty, but deeper. I was concerned that it had changed. I wondered if the healing would be as good. This was my ego thinking. The client always gets what they need and I needed to trust that God is bringing me the vibrational change I need to do the work he has in store for me. I am so grateful God shared the light with me, because with it, he changed my heart. With this new information on healing with Jesus in my heart chakra and using God's light, I don't even feel hot. Instead, I ask my Reiki guides if I am done. It's a totally different sensation, one of relying on the light, and my heart intuition.

February 19, 2016

I woke at 3 am to write down this message from Archangel Gabriel:

World religions have come about due to man's need to believe in God. In search of God, one must go within. God is Love. God lives in your heart.

Love is in all of us. Love does not see color, race, or religion. Think of a time you understood love. Do you remember the feeling coming out of your heart? Do you remember the pure joy, the peace and lightness of your heart? When it felt like all was right with the world? That is God.

God is love, in All of us, All the time. Connect to that joy, peace and lightness in your heart any time you are NOT love. Just stop what you are doing, reconnect to the feeling. Let go of worry or fear that is stopping the love, just give it to God. At first, this takes intense internal concentration. It is worth your time. Once you return to love within, you are rebalanced; mentally, emotionally and physically. Take a few moments to bask in the love feeling. You may need to do this multiple times a day at first. Each time brings you new insights; each time reminds you that you have what it takes within. Each time you concentrate on returning to love or God, the realization that we ALL can do this grows. When more and more people do this, the world energy of LOVE grows.

This is how wars end. THE FEAR IS GONE.

All that is left is God's Love for ALL of us.

March 17, 2016

It took me a long time to be able to discuss this topic publicly, but this is the core of who I am, and what I know for sure (as Oprah would say!). A lot of people consider themselves spiritual, not religious. I am one of those people who attended Catholic services with my Grandmother, had first communion and then only attended as the part time Catholics do- on holidays.

I learned Usui Reiki and it brought me back to my belief in Jesus even stronger than what I learned in church. Church taught me to pray to Jesus, Reiki taught me to heal with him (I Corinthians 12:28-31). The heart centered difference is what I believe most people are looking for today.

I wanted to know God and Jesus internally, not through prayer alone. I wanted to know God and Jesus are with me daily, not just on Sunday. I wanted to know my faith of God and Jesus in my heart not just hear it in my ears. I wasn't getting what I wanted in church.

Reiki brought me back to the more natural path. Be grateful and acknowledge blessings, choose kindness, love more, learn patience and be peace. Yes, the bible talks about all these things, but how do I learn them in the modern day? Everyday life lessons bring about these for consideration. But more and more people are hitting stumbling blocks that don't go away, and are getting bigger instead.

Reiki helped me go inside and learn the value of putting aside emotions to deal only with facts. Reiki helped me stop and smell the roses daily. Reiki helped me realize the value of ALL human life and because of it, choose kindness. Reiki helped me LOVE healing because Jesus is a part of it (John 14:12)! Reiki helped me to be peaceful when everyone around me is falling apart. Reiki is MY answer. IT IS NOT a religion, but certainly helped me reconnect with mine. I don't know if Jesus used "Reiki", but I am convinced Reiki is linked to a form of healing he did use. The similarities are too close not to be related in some way.

I have worked with people of many faiths, and it works with them all! I don't want to dispute religious facts, or change your current belief system; I just want to show you how to enhance what you already love with Reiki! I can tell you I would not be the same person without Reiki!

Sharing the light is my souls purpose....helping you deepen your faith with Reiki is my blessing.

April 18, 2016

One year since Mom passed. I don't know if it's because now I'm the oldest female in the family, but understanding time is different now. I am keenly aware of the limit to time on Earth. Before Mom passed I was urgently in a hurry to get things done because no one knows when time will end. My theory was I should do as much as possible today because I am not sure if I will be here tomorrow. Hurry, Hurry, Hurry was my internal time beat. Work, clean the house, grocery shop. Hurry, Hurry, Hurry. Tend to everyone else's needs; run the gerbil treadmill, HURRY!

Since Mom has passed, life has slowed down. Part of it is sheer energy depletion from emotional changes due to her death. The other part is a clear realization that the things you value and give importance to will always happen. The rest is not important and to stress about it is a waste of time and more importantly, energy. The things that I do I now, I do with the BE HERE NOW mentality. I listen more, judge less, and I try hard to see the good in EVERY THING. Sometimes I have to strain to see it, but it's always there. And above all I see and hear with LOVE. When you see with love, everything has meaning. When you hear with love, everything is important. All the senseless stuff doesn't get me upset any more. I simply walk away from the drama. This enhanced knowing has calmed my heart and allowed me to see the bigger picture.

People are love. Yes, it is hard to see immediately in some people. Everyone is with the people you are with for a reason. We all have something to share to enhance each other's lives. Love lets you see it. Put aside the petty bickering, look for the love. This doesn't mean you should let people take advantage of you in any way. There are still common sense limitations here, but when you look with love you see from a different angle. When you look with love, your understanding is enhanced. The love angle is one that comes from your heart, goes out to another, leaves their heart and comes back to you. Loves shape is the heart, it starts at the bottom point and goes up, into their heart, makes a hook and connects to yours, returning to the bottom point where there is no division. Look for it in every encounter, and you will become a new person.

Mom is still teaching me, I love you!

May 3, 2016

It's 11pm and I feel so much unconditional love that tears are rolling down my face. I ask why I am feeling this way, and receive the following message:

This love you are feeling pouring through you is from Mary. Her love of the World feels this way. It's all engulfing; you feel it in every cell of your body. Imagine walking around like this all the time, it's overwhelming the love she has for all. These feelings of love and joy are to be shared with all humanity. Let them know of her love for all. All we have to do is ask and she will be here for us; guiding us, helping us, loving us. So many want help, just a hug....be there for each other, with kind words, deeds and a shoulder to lean on. This world needs everyone to do their share right where you are. Don't under estimate the smallest deed, kindness or thought. Prayers are heard, and are changing the way the world is opening up to love everywhere. Do not be discouraged by those who don't understand, keep shining on. Share the light, and let it be seen. Mothers' Day is a time to thank Mother Earth for all she has done for us. For the one who sustains life remember to thank her and treat her with respect. She can support you but you need to stand up for her, and take away the chemicals that are poisoning the water, the earth and the air. You only have this one earth, be one with her. Stop on Mothers' Day and honor the grass, trees and air be grateful for the water and all that it provides for you daily. You have all heard it before, but now is the time to wake up and come together before it is too late. Everyone thinks it's not up to them, that they are only one person, but together you are one, the world, Earth is one. You are one. God and you are one and the same, you can be the one! Be the ONE. Be LOVE, Love your Mother, and Mother Earth.

Mother Mary is peace. She brings all the calm that can be brought to earth. She watched over all of us, bringing light and healing and love. Extreme love. Unconditional love. For all, I wish you could feel this. My whole left side from crown to foot is tingly. I need guidance as I know I am supposed to do something great, and I don't know where to go or what to do. I need help. Please Mother Mary, guide me. Thank you.

August 2, 2016

I am over joyed to announce Suli Sullivan, Leonard Diana and I are opening a new healing center! The past few years have been a period of building a solid foundation of the best people in the energy healing business in this area. I now have two executive partners and several other collaborative partners all in this venture together. Years ago, I knew I couldn't accomplish my dream without more experts involved. I am thrilled to announce the name is Sharing the Light Wholistic Center, LLC. in Avon, CT. I have been using the phrase "Sharing the Light" for years and know it is what is most needed in the world today. I know I am being guided to continue to do incredible healing sessions and teach people how to become Reiki Practitioners. One person at a time, I know that more and more people sharing the light will change hearts. It worked for me, and I know it can work for you too! Namaste!

Extra's:

The Quick Guide to explain Reiki:

What is it? Reiki is Universal energy, it is in everything. Just because YOU can't feel or see it doesn't mean it's not there. People who use Reiki feel energy in everything, from a stone to plants and energy coming from people. The energy that is in people can slow down, get stuck and then cause disease. Reiki can get rid of the negative slow energy and replace it to heal your issues! Reiki is an unconditional loving energy, can't ever cause harm and you will be amazed at the extent to which it can and does heal, if YOU allow it.

What Reiki isn't: It's not a religion. Dr. Usui was the one who figured out how to start the energy. It doesn't matter which religion he was, everyone can use it. It won't turn you into a Buddhist. It does make whatever you believe in deeper. By connecting with it, and getting additional energy from it daily, you begin to understand the depth of your beliefs. It takes you deeper into your thoughts about it and brings a new level of commitment to it. Energy is a necessity for everyone. Therefore, everyone can and should use it.

Where do you use it? Anywhere! I have given in person Reiki to people in the grocery store, in malls, hospitals and nursing homes. You can use it in emergencies, by just saying "Reiki now" and it will turn on.

When do you use it? Any time you feel something is not feeling right. YOU know your body best, and when it's off balance, YOU know that too! I suggest you Reiki the issue as soon as you feel it in order to get rid of it quickly. If you wait a few hours, it may take longer to get rid of it as it is deeper in your cellular memory.

You can use it in conjunction with massage for an extremely relaxing modality. People use it with physical therapy, occupational therapy, nursing, and volunteers use Reiki before and or after surgery. Anyone working in a hospital, rehabilitation or veterinarian hospital can use it. And of course, if you are a mom or dad, it's a handy tool in your medicine box! I use it a lot when anyone has a fever or sunburn; it instantly knows when you need cold energy versus hot too!

How does it change your life? It gives a deeper and richer meaning to whatever your soul purpose is, or if you haven't found it, this will put you on the path. When using it daily, there is an intense focus on wanting to be part of the solution to world issues, but it starts helping in your daily life first.

How do you defend it? Many people initially struggle with the people who think it is witchcraft or a religion. I like to go back to the quote I use in my Reiki 1 manual... "There will always be violent opposition from mediocre minds." I explain that if something heals you, and it comes from unconditional love, why wouldn't you continue to do it?

Why do people sit on the fence about it? I know many who didn't think it could possibly help. They'd been to a gazillion doctors and specialists who told them they've tried everything. If the person only "believes" in doctors and the science that back it up, this is truly a hard sell for them. Science is starting to do tests to back up the energy behind it. The science is shown in....an article written by Bernadette Doran, BS, RMT: The Science Behind Reiki. She quotes Dr. Oschman, "the electromagnetic fields produced by a Practitioners hands can induce current flows in the tissues and cells of individuals who are in close proximity." Dr. John Zimmerman measured the magnetic field frequencies of Reiki Practitioners and found that the range was .3 to 30 Hz, the same range of frequencies associated with healthy tissue and organs. Rollin McCraty concludes "the more the healer can focus on a state of sincere love or caring, the more coherent the energy and the greater effect on tissue repair."

Reflection: This is what I know for sure, the people who come from a place of love in their heart are the greatest healers! Now it is proven with science!

Many people believe that GOD/Universe can't heal through people, so for them it will be a difficult road. In my opinion, we are all here for a reason. We live in a certain state to meet others that are here for a reason. If you keep your mind open and look for the reason, you will be amazed at the connections!

There are friends who will listen to your stories and be supportive of you, but still not try it. Sometimes they won't try it for years. This is the toughest case scenario because they are the ones you love, and know if they'd just let you give it to them, they would love it. Then, when they are totally desperate, they give in and let you do it. At this point they have nothing to lose. That's the most favorite part of mine, because the AH-HA moment is beyond AWESOME! THIS IS THE MOMENT I LIVE FOR! I don't know why it is so impossible for some to open their minds to let in this idea. But it is....and then when they understand that it heals deeper each time they get it, the response is normally, "Why didn't you tell me sooner?" Meanwhile, you have been trying all the time!

For those who use it on a daily basis, it changes your ability to know things. Your intuition increases, you can tell when people are lying to you just from the energy you feel while in their presence. When working with such a loving energy, any negativity is easy to "see" as if it is the color black over everything. The negativity can't hide from you because it is drawn to the light, which is you.

When Reiki Practitioners complain about a physical disease I ask: "Have you Reiki'd it?" The number one answer is: "I don't have time." If you are serious about healing naturally, you will find time. The sooner you do it when you need it, the quicker it will heal. What is more important than your health? Don't make your body yell at you with pain for attention, just Reiki it!

Many people don't understand distance Reiki. I explain it is like prayer. When people pray for a certain person to heal from surgery, it helps them heal quicker. Prayer is a conversation with God to heal a certain person. Reiki is prayer in the sense that you are working with God to heal someone. The difference is that you get permission from the person to heal them. The person sending Reiki is working on a soul level, to heal the original wound. When you heal at this level, it is gone. This takes practice to do. You are simply asking questions to find out the issue, while asking God to heal it. Remember when you call a person's "I AM" presence, you get their soul. I once had someone call my I AM presence to help her heal another. This is tricky as you don't want any negative energy to attach to you. Be sure to make it known on a daily basis during your prayers that you allow positive energies to go to people, you allow positive energies into you, but no negative or lower vibrational energies to come into you. The words you use are extremely important, be sure that this is a part of your daily intentions.

Love and intention is what makes healing happen. I'm not talking about a simple prayer. This is a heart to heart talk with your God/Universe as to what you would like for your highest and greatest good. That doesn't mean you can ask for excellent health and continue smoking. You have to make the effort to change for the request to be activated. Life proceeds out of intention. When I wanted a new house, I researched house plans, figured out rules of contractors, looked at lots and investigated land. There's a lot to do behind the scenes to prove you are serious about building a new house. Then when the money was being discussed, I simply said to God, if it is meant to be, let us find the right location at the price we can afford, and we did. Reiki is similar. Know what chakra is bothering you, figure out which stones can help, what color you should wear, which codes to use, apply Reiki every moment you get, ask God, Archangels and spirit guides to continually help, ask the questions related to that chakra and do the hard work. Intention takes constant intense concentration in the change you want to see/heal. It's not a do it once and then be upset because it didn't work. You need to apply it every chance you get, be seriously committed about the healing you want, and believe it will happen. I have done it on myself, opened myself up and poured my heart out to the Divine and know that this is how it works. Reiki IT!

Many people ask if they have to believe in God in order for Usui Reiki to work for/on them. The answer is no, you don't have to believe. I Believe. I am simply the channel for the Reiki to pass thru me to you for YOUR highest and greatest good/healing. Whatever it is that you need, you will receive. I have worked on an atheist with extreme pain and once the client found out that I believed in God, the pain which had disappeared returned. What did that tell me? That even though the pain was enough for the client to seek alternative treatment, his mind was still not quite open enough to making progress on his personal path.

Favorite stones in no particular order:

Selenite: I have often said, "If I could only have one stone, it would be selenite!" This stone assists me in removing any negative energy in clients during Reiki sessions. After the session is over I use it to remove negative energy from myself. I use it to clear any other stone by putting them on the selenite. I have a huge peach selenite slab that I use under my feet to ground me. I want to buy more to sit on as well to be able to hold some, sit on some and put my feet on some. It is amazing!

Peach aventurine- I had a Reiki treatment with this on my heart chakra- (peach is the higher heart color) and I felt heaviness like someone pushing down on my chest. I slept with it that night and my heart thumped loudly, and then settled me into a great night's sleep. This particular stone had an angel in it, and it was gone in the am. I am hoping she is now inside my heart!

The most amazing stone for answers is the gold sheen black obsidian. When I ask it specific questions I get answers in the form of pictures. One of my dearest friends husband was extremely ill and I asked it to show me what was going on with him. I was shown a mom and dad holding a baby. I thought, great he is going to be fine, and they will have another child. Then a voice told me it's his parents (who had passed) waiting for their baby. OH my goodness….my heart was filled with sadness and I couldn't stop crying. Then I thought, maybe this is wrong….it's just a stone. He passed 10 days later. This stone has never been wrong, and I use it only in situations where I feel a need to know something that is extremely important.

Chinese Writing Rock- mine is black with green markings and is always sitting by me while writing. I find it is helpful to make the writing go smoother, the words come easier, and the process quicker!

Labradorite and Purple Flourite is excellent for third eye expansion and is recommended for anyone wanting to open it during Reiki 1 class.

Blue Kyanite is always used during Reiki sessions. It quickly opens chakras, making the Reiki sessions go so much quicker! I have a piece of green kyanite I use for my personal heart chakra. It is recommended for those with anemia, or any heart issue.

Clear quartz- I have them in pyramid, heart, round and merkaba shapes! They amplify any other stone you are using it with! You can never have too many of these in my opinion! I also use have a piece on every corner of my Reiki table as a grid before the client arrives.

Amethyst- I have a huge one that was a part of A Hand in Healing when I purchased it, and it will always be with me! It is excellent to lay down in front of while meditating!

Lapis Lazuli and Herkimer Diamond- For DNA repair, everyone needs it!

Angelite and Celestite for connecting to angels!

Kambaba, Icelandic Spar and Mookite- for menopause

Lionskin- stone of wealth and grounding

Prehnite- stone of prophecy

Green Tree Agate- protection in cars and for success and prosperity

Rose quartz and Kunzite- spirtitual stones, unconditional love

Red jasper- the first stone I purchased to balance me, as I need the number 6 vibration which is missing in my name!

To program crystals/stones with Reiki:

Each crystal can hold thousands of prayers of intention at a time and you can add the intentions as you think of them.

Use the counter clock wise Cho Ku Rei, and then Sei He Ki to clear your stone, repeat until you feel it is done. Typically it needs to be done three times to clear it and three times to program it. Then tell it the use you would like it to help you with and program it with clockwise Cho Ku

Rei and Hon Sha Ze Sho Nen for healing. Ask it to be self-cleansing and not to channel any energy that is not of Divine unconditional love. Ask it not to allow anyone else to be able to change the program. You can ask it for help with business, classes, and teachings or just bring more love into your life. The possibilities are endless!

Vibrational number information From Melody's book: <u>Love is in the Earth</u>. You can find out the vibrational number you are missing in your name. Numbers that are excluded from your name are those vibrations that are needed during this lifetime. Each rock/stone has numerical vibration; you simply buy stones that are the vibration you need. You carry them with you in your pockets, wear them as jewelry and sleep with them in your pillow case. This is how I found out I needed red jasper, I need the number 6!

How do you pick a stone? I typically can see the stone almost yell out to me to buy it! If that is not happening for you yet, pick up each one and place it in the center of your hand. Have a mental conversation with it and ask it to let you know if it wants to go home with you. The stone will get hot, cold or tingly in your hand, and you will know it's the one!

I believe our names can reveal vibrations that are missing as numbers, and I believe the following numerical codes can also assist in healing. From Doctors with Reiki, I have used these codes with huge success:

From Doctors with Reiki

http://Reikidoc.blogspot.com/2014/06/divine-healing-codes-and-how-to-use-them.html

Healing The Chakras with codes:

First Chakra (Red or Root)

13 23 251 to optimize and balance the energy of the base or 'root' chakra (red)

10 010 5856 for chronic root chakra blockage/inability to ground to Gaia

Second Chakra (Orange or Navel)

54 28 131 to optimize and balance the energy of the second or 'sacral' chakra (orange)

Third Chakra (Yellow or Solar Plexus)

80 03 011 to optimize and balance the energy of the third or 'solar plexus' chakra (yellow)

Fourth Chakra (Green or Heart)

54 56 821 to optimize and balance the energy of the fourth or 'heart' chakra (green)

88 76 543 for opening the heart chakra when it is closed--good for low self-esteem, lack of self-love, poor self-acceptance, and deep injuries on a soul-level. It will not resolve karmic imbalance but it supports the healing process greatly. Use with permission from your Higher Self or Inner Guidance for you, and also with permission on a soul level if used to help heal another.

Fifth Chakra (Blue or Throat)

77 74 089 to optimize and balance the energy of the fifth or 'throat' chakra (blue)

88 26 789 for opening the throat chakra for better communication ability (use only with the permission from your Higher Self and intuitive guide each time it is used--there is risk of a side effect of energy 'jam' that might need to be released by a Reiki Master in the person who uses it without this permission. It is powerful, this code.)

Sixth Chakra (Indigo or Pituitary)

82 88 133 to optimize and balance the energy of the sixth or 'third eye' chakra (indigo)

Seventh Chakra (White or Crown)

10 01 688 to optimize and balance the energy of the seventh or 'crown' chakra (white)

Higher Chakras (Silver, Gold or Master Chakra)

34 50 824 to optimize and balance the energy of the master chakra (all)

References

Ted Andrews, Animal-Speak, The Spiritual & Magical Powers of Creatures Great & Small (St. Paul, MN, Llewellyn Publications, 2001)

Debbie Ford, The Dark Side of the Light Chasers (Riverhead Books, November 2010)

John Harvey Gray and Lourdes Gray, Hand to Hand the Longest-Practicing Reiki Master Tells His Story (USA, 2002)

Barbara M. Hardie, Soul Releasement Assisting Souls into the Light(MA, Crystal Clear Publishing, 2013)

Barbara M. Hardie, Creating Heaven on Earth- A Guide to Personal Ascension(MA, Crystal Clear Publishing, 2011)

Claire Heartsong, Anna, Grandmother of Jesus A Message of Wisdom and Love (USA, S.E.E. Publishing Company, 2002)

International Center for Reiki Training, An Evidence Based History of Reiki (MI, International Center for Reiki Training, 2015)

Denise Linn, Sacred Space, Clearing and Enhancing the Energy of Your Home (New York, Ballantine Books, 1995)

Melody, Love is in the Earth (CO, Earth-Love Publishing House, 1995)

Karyn Mitchell, Ph.D., Reiki A Torch in Daylight (IL, Mind Rivers Publications, 1994)

Carolin Myss, Ph.D., Anatomy of the Spirit, The Seven Stages of Power and Healing (NY, Three Rivers Press, 1996)

Cheryl Roby, The Roby Chart, 2004

Baird T. Spalding, Life and Teaching of the Masters of the Far East (CA, DeVorss & Company, 1955)

Bernie Siegel, MD, Peace, Love and Healing (Harper Paperbacks, 2011)

Diane Stein, Essential Reiki, A Complete Guide to an Ancient Healing Art (CA, The Crossing Press, Inc., 1996)

Diane Stein, Essential Psychic Healing, A Complete Guide to Healing Yourself, Healing Others, and Healing the Earth (CA, Crossing Press, 2006)

James F. Twyman, The Moses Code (USA, Hay House, Inc., 2008)

Alberto Villoldo, Ph.D., Illumination, The Shaman's Way of Healing (United States: Hay House, 2010)

Donald Neale Walsh, Conversations with God (Berkley, 1995)

About the Author

Rev. Cheryl-Ann M. Case is a traditional Usui Reiki Master Teacher since 2001. She is owner of Southington Reiki, LLC dba A Hand in Healing in CT. Cheryl is also a certified Lightarian AngelLinks facilitator, and works with Seraph Rose Aura and Archangels Michael, Raphael, Gabriel and Uriel on a daily basis in conjunction with Reiki. Cheryl is an Approved Provider for Continuing Education with the National Certification Board for Therapeutic Massage and Bodywork and a member of the International Association of Reiki Professionals. In appreciation, a portion of this books profit will be donated to the American Red Cross.